To dear Brett

Love,

Evelyn

WHAT HAPPENS WHEN GOD ANSWERS

Evelyn Christenson

Foreword by Charles Colson

WHAT HAPPENS WHEN GOD ANSWERS

WORD BOOKS
PUBLISHER
WACO, TEXAS
A DIVISION OF
WORD, INCORPORATED

Library of Congress Cataloging in Publication Data
Christenson, Evelyn.
  What happens when God answers.

  1. Prayer. I. Title.
BV220.C47 1986   248.3′2   86–11128
ISBN 0–8499–0569–9

67898BKC98764321

Printed in the United States of America

Through the long difficult months of living through and writing this book, my four precious granddaughters have filled my life with sparkle and joy. God's timing in sending them to us was incredible, as their hugs and affection have charged my whole being with new life and motivation.

So this happy grandmother dedicates this book to those four little girls:

Cynthia Joy Thompson
Jennifer Diane Johnson
Crista Alisse Johnson
Kathleen Mae Thompson

CONTENTS

FOREWORD

"Our ultimate goal is to be engulfed by an attitude of gratitude," Evelyn Christenson writes toward the end of this splendid book. She is writing about an attitude of thanksgiving toward the Lord that should mark everything we do. But I don't mind saying that Evelyn herself fills me with an attitude of gratitude. I am grateful for the privilege of being able to know her well over these years, grateful for her ministry, and grateful to the Lord for giving us the opportunity to work together as board members of Prison Fellowship.

This is one of those rare books that tells us something of what God is like. Mrs. Christenson begins with a simple question: What happens when God answers our prayers? She doesn't say *if* God answers our prayers; she assumes He answers them, as indeed He does. Neither does she have in mind a crude cause-and-effect relationship: we ask for something, God gives it to us—or He doesn't. For her, prayer is something more subtle and complex. It opens a door; it shows us a way. When she asks, "What happens when God answers?" she is asking a basic and somewhat frightening question. What happens when we walk in the door—and discover that the Master of the universe is speaking to us, directing us, making demands of us?

He tells us many things—that we need to pray more, that we've been praying the wrong prayer, that we need to search the Scriptures, that we need to grow in holiness, or even that our prayer has already been answered.

Very often—and this is where I find Evelyn Christenson's book most challenging—God answers our prayers by telling us to change the way we relate to Him and to the people we love. Do we pray for grace to overcome an area of weakness? The Lord will tell us to get on our knees and repent. Do we pray for a wayward spouse or an unbelieving child? The Lord might tell us to serve that person to the limit of our strength. Do we pray for grace and wisdom? The Lord will give it—and then commission us to spill out our lives in the work of sharing the Good News with the unsaved.

It can be a fearsome thing to pray. We might fall into the hands of the living God. Evelyn Christenson has no illusions about how difficult it is to follow Him.

Yet, as I read this book, I kept thinking to myself, "Hard as it is, who would want to live any other way?" So often we go through our days and weeks and months with our heads filled with *our* plans; instead, we need to live *His* way, with *His* way to love, *His* way to serve, *His* way to think. His ways are not our ways—and that is a relief. Our Father in heaven has revealed a better way to live. How good it is to be freed from the burden of our own ideas.

The gateway to this freedom is prayer. Evelyn Christenson has tirelessly devoted her life to showing us how to open this door to freedom. Because of her ministry—and because of the prayer support of many of her friends and associates—thousands of people all over the world know how to pray. In this book, they will learn what happens when God answers.

That is enough reason to read this book. But there is another reason. By reading it, you will get to know my friend Evelyn Christenson—a woman who embodies the lifestyle of prayer in her own life. Evelyn herself has discovered what happens when God answers. She willingly shares this discovery with us, just as she has willingly spent her whole life serving the God she loves.

CHARLES W. COLSON

PREFACE

Because eighteen years have passed since our original experimentation in prayer, which produced the book *What Happens When Women Pray*, it seemed only right to take a good, honest look at what really *did* happen. The magnitude of what we have seen God do in answer to those years of praying is in this book.

Starting with a committee of eight women in Rockford, Illinois, in 1968, God has exploded this ministry across America and overseas. I personally have taught hundreds of thousands in all denominations to pray here in the United States and around the world. And millions have read that book, studied it, and taught it. Prayer groups and chains have formed in all kinds of churches, organizations, in whole cities, and even in some entire countries.

Through the years, we have concentrated on the *human perspective* of prayer—learning to obey the scriptural prerequisites to power in prayer and then discovering the power of our prayers. Now, this book contains what we have learned about *God's perspective* of prayer. What He expects to happen *with* His answers. What happens to us and through us *after* He answers.

We have learned that an answer to prayer is not an end in itself, but it is always God's opening of the next door of our lives and ushering us into the next era He has for us.

Prayer is one of God's chief means of accomplishing His will on planet earth. Here is the way we have discovered He does it!

1

WHEN GOD ANSWERS . . .

Here Is My Perspective

When God answers a prayer, it is not the final closing curtain on an episode in our lives. Rather, it is the opening of the curtain to the next act. The most important part of prayer is what we do with God's answers and how His answers affect us.

God never intends that an answer to prayer be an end in itself. He expects much more than an emotional response—joy, disappointment, or anger—to His answer. He expects us to be prepared to act or to be acted upon by His answer to our prayers.

God's answer to a prayer is His means of accomplishing His will here on earth. The way He answers reveals to us His sovereign will, His plan, His reasoning, and His perspective on the subject. We must ask, "What does God expect to accomplish *with* this answer?"

God's Intentions

We seem to place so much emphasis on our prayer requests, and then on God's answers, that we forget what He intends us to do *with* His answer. Most of us pray a specific prayer, receive an answer—whether or not it is to our liking—and consider the case closed. In our prayer notebooks, we write down the request, and then opposite it—with joyous or resigned finality—record the answer when it comes. But God does not consider the case closed. He opens a whole new arena of action by the answer He gives. Our response to His answer should be, "What next, Lord?"

According to Jeremiah 33:3, there is another step, something *after* the prayer and *after* the answer:

> "Call unto me, and I will answer thee, and show thee great and mighty things, which thou knowest not."

God's time-tested promise to Jeremiah is in three parts, not our usual two-part approach of "our calling" and "His answering."

Rarely does God stamp "case closed" when He answers one of our prayers. Rather, it is often what happens after God answers that is life-changing.

"Which Thou Knowest Not"

Have you ever wished that you could get a glimpse into God's mind? The God who ordained all the physical laws of space and time? The God who designed all the minute details of an incredibly complex universe? The God in whom all things consist and operate? There is a way. It is possible to perceive what is in the mind of the omniscient God of the universe. How? By examining His answers to your prayers!

In our prayer ministry, we have been continuously surprised at God's "things we did not know." As we have experimented for twenty-one years with ever-enlarging amounts and methods of prayer, God has surprised us with so much more than that for which we asked. I am constantly amazed that God does not limit answering our prayers because of our inability to ask.

The exciting thing is that the last phrase of Jeremiah 33:3 refers to things we know nothing about—not ideas we dreamed up or plans we devised. As I look back over my life of prayer, this pattern becomes so obvious. I ask God for just one thing, and He keeps on answering long after I even recognize it as His response to my prayer.

Months before my first prayer seminar in war-torn Belfast, Northern Ireland, in June of 1981, our prayer chains "called unto God" in prayer for my safety, for those whom He wanted to attend, and for His power in the seminar. Then when He started answering, we praised Him that, after the registrations were filled to the capacity of one thousand people, others called, crying and pleading over the phone, "We must come to learn to pray, for the only hope for our country is prayer."

As God continued to answer prayer at the seminar, the pray-ers thanked Him that the large downtown Presbyterian Hall had been engaged and was filled—by both Catholics and Protestants who were at war! In awe, we praised Him as members of these opposing factions held hands in their groups and asked God to forgive them as they forgave each other. Many actually trembled as they prayed together. And the pray-ers almost burst with praise when at the close they all held hands and sang, "Blest be the tie that binds our hearts in Christian love." How thrilled we were that seven hundred from both sides signed up for combined telephone prayer chains in Northern Ireland. And then with prayers of relief and thanksgiving, my husband, Chris, and I were whisked out of Ireland safely after the seminar. We called unto God, and He certainly did answer.

But I wonder how many of those pray-ers then turned to the "Belfast Prayer Seminar" page, dated June 9, 1981, in their prayer request notebook and mentally stamped "case closed" on that page?

God's Continued Involvement

God, however, did not stamp the case "closed." He continued to work after those initial answers and accomplished "great and mighty things, which [we knew] not."

God left the situation open-ended so that He could expand those seven hundred pray-ers into prayer chains and groups all over Northern Ireland—so that He could use those Irish pray-ers, along with others, to reach Liam and Jimmy, two imprisoned terrorists from opposite sides of the Irish "religious war"—so that two years later, I could sit and listen spellbound as I interviewed Liam during our Prison Fellowship International Symposium in Belfast, a part of Charles Colson's ministry.

Liam was a boyish-looking Catholic inmate furloughed from prison for a few days to attend our symposium. How privileged I felt that he had saved a couple of hours just to talk with me. As I sat with my mind riveted on his incredible story, Liam told me that as an IRA terrorist he had been arrested and imprisoned for ten years. He spoke of the blanket protests when IRA inmates refused to wear the British clothing issued to them. He shuddered as he recounted their "dirty" protests when they refused to wash and threw their own excrement against the walls of their cells. Then, quietly, he spoke of his own hunger strike. The limp in his walk was a painful reminder of its devastation on his muscles.

Liam told me that as the last person on the Bobby Sands' hunger strike in the Maze Prison, near Belfast, he was blind and dying after fifty-six days without food and had slipped into a coma. It was his mother who then insisted on his being fed intravenously, thus ending the series of ten young prisoners who had starved themselves to death for their cause. (Later, I squeezed that dear, brave Irish mother as she stood beaming at her son's side at our symposium.)

After recovering from his horrible experience of being just hours from death, Liam found himself in a solitary confinement cell. "All they would let me have," he told me, "was a Bible. And while I read that Bible and . . ." He paused, slowly and deliberately enunciating his next words, *"because all those people were praying for me*—I accepted Jesus as my Savior."

Also attending that symposium was a Protestant prisoner named Jimmy, who, although on the opposite side of the conflict, had watched Liam's transformed life. And Jimmy, wanting what Liam had, also accepted Christ. Now the two are in Magilligan Prison, studying the Bible together in the same study group and meeting on a regular basis to pray together. Liam told me that if he had seen Jimmy before finding Christ, he would have "shot him dead" (not a stretch of the truth). "But now," said Liam, "I would die for Jimmy."

Our final Prison Fellowship rally at Queens University in Belfast was open to the public—both Catholics and Protestants who were still at war. As Liam and Jimmy stood together on the platform radiating and sharing their mutual love for Jesus, the whole crowd erupted in a thunderous standing ovation, weeping together and hugging each other throughout the huge auditorium.

God had used the prayers for a seminar, perhaps in a small way, to help accomplish some of His will for that war-torn country. And He will continue to answer, fulfilling Liam's words to me, "My hope is to believe that God is changing the hearts of men like myself and Jimmy. And that's the only hope I have for peace in my country, Northern Ireland."

Yes, each answer to prayer is God's opening of the door to what He intends to accomplish next in this world. With the answer to the initial prayer comes the continuation of God's involvement. But we may not recognize it as such; we may even forget that we prayed or, even worse, take for granted that what is happening is just the natural course of events. "Great and mighty things, which thou knowest not."

God's Surprises

My prayer ministry has been full of God's surprises—great and mighty things He did over and above that for which we prayed. In fact, I have experienced a continuing shock in my prayer seminars. God has been showing me what I call His *hidden mission field.* And no matter how frequently I see it, I am still surprised. I did not seek to find it; in fact, I really did not know the extent to which it existed. But God has shown me a *hidden mission field* existing right inside Christian churches around the world. This mission field is made up of church members who are not sure whether they know Jesus personally as Savior and Lord.

I first experienced this shock when I started my overseas ministry. Teaching my first prayer seminars in Australia in 1980, I found that most of the attendees already belonged to well-respected churches and were regularly studying the Bible with my sponsors, an international women's Bible study organization. However, when I asked all who were not sure of their personal relationship with Jesus to pray aloud together in their groups of four—to my utter amazement—approximately a fourth of them prayed, accepting Jesus for the first time or making sure of their salvation.

This pattern has continued wherever I have gone—in the audience of Protestants and Catholics in Ireland, in Scotland and all across England; next in Taiwan, Japan, India, and back through the British Isles. Then home in America, to my amazement, the percentage began to rise.

The usual 5 percent and then 10 percent praying the prayer of commitment in my seminars hadn't surprised me too much, but when the percentage suddenly soared to 25 percent and above, I was stunned. It seemed incomprehensible that so large a portion of those coming to learn to pray were not sure whether they had a personal relationship with Jesus. And most incredible was the fact that almost everyone who attends my seminars here and abroad already is a member of a respectable church.

In the past two years, the statistics have risen to 50 percent quite frequently, and even as high as 75 percent several times, making the average almost one-half of our audiences praying this prayer.

Wondering if I was exaggerating these statistics, after my last seminar, I shared my concern with the host pastor who had been on the platform with me. "How many would you estimate prayed aloud today, making sure they knew Jesus as Savior and Lord?" I asked.

"Oh, well over half!" he exclaimed with profound joy. God's surprises of "things which thou knowest not"!

God's Perspective of Prayer Answers

But there are other kinds of surprises from God when He answers our prayers. I have discovered how "unhuman" God's ways of thinking really are. Things that seem so right, so good, so timely, so logical, so obvious to us frequently are refused, replaced, and even reversed by God as He—without ever making a mistake, missing the mark, being too early or too late—fields the answers out of His omniscient mind.

We need to see prayer from God's perspective. We should try to see the big picture of what God's overall plan might be; and how each little and big request with His answer fits into His sovereign purpose. How often we question when God doesn't answer the way we wanted. How we grumble when we think He has not answered, when actually we have not recognized His answer. Or, when in rebellion, we decide that if this is how God is going to answer, we are never going to pray again.

But God has told us the "great and mighty things" He would do after His answer were "things we know not." God's omniscient thought process determines His answer to the prayers His earthly children pray, as well as all things those answers initiate.

Also, God's answer usually precipitates expanded and more fervent prayers from us. With His answer, we find ourselves on the next plateau from which we then launch our next endeavor through prayer.

How often we hear, "God always answers, but His answers are yes, no, or wait." In my own experience, I have not found God's answers to be that simplistic. His interaction with me in prayer is much more complex and far-reaching. His answer always includes, "Keep interacting with Me, My child. I have much I want to accomplish through your prayers."

Our Response to God's Answers

People respond in various ways to God's answers to their prayers. There are many different responses to prayer recorded in the New Testament. There is the choice of *witnessing*. Anna prayed for many years to see the Messiah; and when God answered her prayers at baby Jesus' circumcision, she went out and told everyone she had seen the Messiah. But Simeon's response was quite different. After praying the same prayer for a similar time period, he, too, saw the Messiah. But his response was, "Now I am ready to die."

There is also the reaction of *disbelief*. When the early Christians were praying for Peter's release from prison, they could not believe that God really had answered their prayers, thinking it was his ghost knocking at the gate. There is the response of *obedience*. Peter's prayers on the rooftop were answered by God in a vision he did not understand at the time. But even so, when God did explain it, Peter obeyed immediately and brought the gospel to the Gentiles.

We have to make a *choice*. Paul and Silas prayed and sang in the prison, and God answered by sending an earthquake that opened all the doors and broke the prisoners' chains.

But Paul chose to forego the immediate freedom in order to win the jailor to Christ. Perhaps one of the most difficult responses to God's answer to fervent prayer came from Paul. It was the response of *acceptance.* Paul prayed three times for his thorn in the flesh to be removed, but he accepted God's answer—no—and settled down to a life of promised power, strength, and sufficient grace.

The Bible reveals myriads of different responses to God when He answered prayer—some good, some bad, some rebellious, some submissive, some joyous, some thankful, some angry. Our responses to God's answers to our prayers can be many and varied also. The decision is up to us.

Ushered Into

The decision as to our response will determine the next state of our spiritual condition, attitude, relationship with God, or arena of activity. Every prayer request, no matter how large or small, always ushers us into our next state. We pray, God answers, and we then decide what to do with His answer.

Through all His answers, God's desires are always that we step into the next room of forgiveness, joy, Christlikeness, peace, power, and fruit bearing. And, if necessary, His answer includes our being restored to this state. But we must accept His answer.

But God's answer may have to include the steps He knows are necessary to answer our original prayer. So, rather than looking at a once-for-all answer to a prayer, we must look to what must happen after God answers to produce His ultimate answer. We usually can expect a series of more prayers and more answers that are generated by our first prayer, and then each subsequent prayer.

Since God's answer is always that which ultimately will produce what is absolutely best for the pray-er, we must be willing for His intermediary answers. They are the stepping stones He knows are essential to His ushering us into that eventual end state He desires for us.

Opening the Curtain

Jesus said in Matthew 7:7, "Knock, and it shall be opened unto you." What will be opened? Whatever God has for you!

His next open door. A better life with Him. God is using the prayers you are praying today to open the curtain to the rest of your life.

Closing Prayer

Oh, God, I deeply desire to understand Your perspective of prayer. Please teach me how I should respond to Your answers to my prayers so that You can direct my life through them.

In Jesus' name, **Amen.**

2

WHEN GOD ANSWERS . . .

I Am Not Able

How do we handle God's answer to a prayer when He says, "I am not able. Capable? Yes. Able? No."

How shocking it is when, although we are praying for something we know is His will, God answers, "My child, I am not able!" Then He explains, "It is true that I am capable of everything. It is true that I have more power than the combined power of all the things I have created. Yes, it is true that I am capable of doing 'exceeding abundantly above all [you] ask or think' [see Eph. 3:20], but as to answering that prayer, I am not able!"

Even while longing to answer yes to our prayer requests and when eager to usher us into that next open door or condition, there are times He must answer: "I am not able."

God taught me this as I stopped in California for a prayer seminar en route home from Taiwan. After spending much time in deep intercessory prayer that morning, I had asked God to bring to my mind the Scripture He had for me for that day's seminar. Ephesians 3:20 instantly flashed across my mind. I silently recited it over and over:

"Now unto him that is able to do exceeding abundantly above all that we ask or think, according to the power that worketh in us."

According To

But as I repeated the verse over and over, only two words kept standing out: *according to, according to.* I puzzled over what God was trying to teach me. The verse suddenly seemed so complicated; I decided to break it down. I lumped the words "exceeding abundantly above all that we ask or think" into a simple "all that." God can do "all that." Then it read, "Now unto him that is able to do . . . all that . . . according to the power that worketh in us." I had it! God is able to do "all that" *only* according to the power that works in us!

Then I really began to ponder this in my heart. I asked myself, "Don't I have God's power in me all the time?" I must have, for as a Christian, all three persons of the Trinity dwell in me. I have Christ in me, "the hope of glory" (Col. 1:27); the Father will come and dwell in us (1 John 4:12–15); and Jesus promised that the Holy Spirit would be in us (John 14:17). In fact, just before Paul's doxology in Ephesians 3, which includes verse 20, he prayed that the Christians at Ephesus would "be filled with all the fulness of God" (Eph. 3:19).

The next question loomed, But do I always have the same amount of God's power working in me? From years of experience, I knew automatically that the answer was no. I do not have the same proportion of God's power all of the time. And He is able to do only in accordance with, in proportion to, the measure of that power which is working in me!

God Limits Himself

Slowly, I saw it. God has the ability to *limit* the amount of power He releases in me. Although I have within me that divine force, the triune God, who is capable of anything and everything, He chooses the amount of power that He will unleash in me. Yes, God can do all He wants to do, but He sets limits as to how much power He will "work in us."

I couldn't wait to get home to check the accuracy of this theology in my reference books. And there it was in many places, including this quote in the old Cambridge Bible commentary, "In the saint [true believer] . . . resides already a Divine force capable in itself of the mightiest developments. To attain these, not a new force, but a fuller application of *this* force, is required." [1] According to!

Augustus Strong wrote, "God can do all He will, but He will not do all He can. Else His power is mere force acting necessarily, and God [would be] the slave of His own omnipotence. God is not compelled to do all He can do, but uses as much of His power as He pleases. Just because He is omnipotent, He does not have to do all He can do." [2]

Still not satisfied, I phoned Berkley Mickelsen, a professor of New Testament Greek at Bethel Seminary, and asked him if my thinking was correct. "Evelyn," he replied, "that seemingly unimportant prepositional phrase 'according to' is the crux of that time-tested doxology of Paul's prayer in Ephesians. You have discovered the most crucial phrase in that verse. Most people never see it." Well, I hadn't seen it either. It was God who showed it to me so clearly that morning in California as I was returning from Taiwan.

Yes, the extent of what God is able to do in us in answer to our prayers depends on, is according to, the measure of power that is working in us. God is capable of all things— but is able to do only according to the amount of power working in us!

We Limit God

What is it, then, that releases greater amounts of God's power? Our prayers, of course! God sends His power in response to adequate praying.

God, through His answers, accomplishes what He has wanted to do all along but has been hindered by our lack of prayer. And although He is sovereign and can and does

---

1. J. J. S. Perowne, ed., *The Cambridge Bible for Schools and Colleges* (London: C. J. Clay and Sons, 1895), p. 102.
2. Augustus Hopkins Strong, *Systematic Theology* (Philadelphia: Judson Press, n.d.), pp. 287–88.

do as He chooses without the help of believers' prayers, He has chosen to operate extensively in response to them.

In 1973, I was one of eleven people who organized six thousand prayer groups in the Minneapolis-St. Paul area for the upcoming Billy Graham Crusade in August of that year. We were expecting—and had—fifty thousand people in attendance. Before leaving my home to train the St. Paul pray-ers one Saturday morning, I noticed that our local newspaper carried the headline, "Billy Graham Has 500,000 First Night in Korea." Shocked, I reported this to our pray-ers and asked why we were aiming at only fifty thousand. But I knew the reason for the difference and gave them the answer. It was all the prayer that the Korean Christians consistently practice. Since the early part of this century, thousands have been going to their churches to pray daily before breakfast; every Friday night, all night, finds tens of thousands in several different prayer meetings, and they solve their problems and intercede in cubicles on their prayer mountains.

At the National Religious Broadcasters Convention in 1985, I was overwhelmed at the display of electronic equipment. Later in the day, in the workshop I was conducting, I asked the people this question: "Are you depending on this tremendous wattage from your transmitters *for* power, or are you sending your message of Jesus *with* power? With all your super transmitting power, are your broadcasts still powerless because of lack of prayer for them?"

Then I had to ask myself the same question. In our daily broadcasts to all of China, are we depending on Trans World Radio's unbelievably powerful transmitters to get our prayer message *to* that one-fourth of the world, or are we sending it *with* God's power—through prayer?

People frequently ask me how much time they should spend in personal closet praying. I reply, "That depends on how much power you want." E. M. Bounds in his book *Power through Prayer* explained, "Our short prayers owe their point and efficiency to the long ones that have preceded them. The short, prevailing prayer cannot be prayed by one who has not prevailed with God in a mightier struggle of long continuance." [3] So, even though God can do anything He

---

3. E. M. Bounds, *Power through Prayer* (Grand Rapids, Mich.: Zondervan Publishing House, 1964), p. 35.

wants, He has chosen to permit us to limit many of His actions by our lack of faithfulness in prayer. Conversely, our sufficient praying will enable Him to give the answers we both desire.

God, with all the power of the universe, is sitting on His throne in glory, even today, waiting and longing to release that power on planet earth. With absolute unlimited power at His disposal (in fact, He *is* unlimited power), He is ready to pull aside the curtain and let us step into a new era of that power in our lives—appropriated by and released through prayer!

Since I found Jesus Christ personally at age nine, I've diligently prayed for others and myself. And I have depended on God's power through prayer in my whole life of ministry. What I have felt all of these years was summed up in January 1982, when I wrote in the margin of my Bible, beside 1 Corinthians 2:4, "This is what I want for my ministry: *'And my message and my preaching were not in persuasive words of wisdom, but in demonstration of the Spirit and of power'* " (NASB, emphasis mine). God has been faithful in sending that power in answer to the prayers of thousands of faithful pray-ers.

Released by Prayer

As I reflected on my trip to Taiwan after receiving God's "according to," I realized the whole thing had been an "Ephesians 3:20 experience." Throughout it all, we had seen an unusual demonstration of God's power released in answer to a tremendous amount of prayer.

Thousands were praying individually, in telephone prayer chains, in groups, and on my twenty-four-hour prayer clock. When I minister overseas, my prayer clock operates continuously. Faithful pray-ers across the United States sign up for specific prayer periods, with the result that many people are on their knees around the clock, day and night, in uninterrupted prayer for my ministry.

There had been just one day between Christmas and my departure for Taiwan. On Christmas night, the last of our guests left at 11:00 o'clock; and in one day, I had to put away the stacks of gifts and wrappings and the best dishes and silver, store all the leftover food, and get my husband ready for his trip to Florida and myself ready for the flight to Taiwan.

In addition, the clothes dryer repairman had come just as our family was about to open gifts on Christmas Eve, leaving the clothes we needed for our trips heaped in the laundry room baskets!

With all the preparations, by the middle of that afternoon, I couldn't go on. Emotionally and physically exhausted, I went into my bathroom, shut the door, and cried. "Lord, I can't go to Taiwan. Look at me. I'm a basket case!" I didn't have to tell the Lord that—He already knew it! But I knew I had to go to Taiwan. So I stoically ironed Chris's shirts and packed.

In sheer determined obedience, I went to the airport the next day. As I slowly trudged down the ramp to the airplane, reluctantly dragging my tote bag behind me, I kept complaining inwardly, "I can't go. I can't go to Taiwan." But just a few feet from the plane, something happened. It was just as if something came right down from heaven and enwrapped me like a blanket. And suddenly, I was filled with excitement, anticipation, strength—and power!

I stopped dead still on the ramp and exclaimed under my breath, "What happened?" And then I remembered. "Oh, this is the day the twenty-four-hour clock starts praying for me!" And, had there not been an airplane at the end of that ramp, I felt as if I could have flown all the way to Taiwan—on my own power!

When God Answers: "I Am Able"

When there is enough prayer, God is able!

Was the only power He released on that Taiwan trip for my personal strength? Oh, no. In Taipei alone, we had participants from forty-three different Christian organizations and church affiliations, a "first" on that island for this kind of unity in women's ministry. A missionary there told me, "Statistically, Taiwan is the most idolatrous nation in the world. The seminars were a light in that dark and pagan country. Such love was manifested there. The women even held hands and prayed together." "The non-Christians," she continued, "brought by Christian friends and family members were overwhelmed by the love shown." So God's answer to much praying began to break a barrier that had been there for many years.

Then God began to melt away a centuries-old tradition in that part of the world to save face. Jeanne Swanson, the missionary responsible for my coming, had said to me, "Evelyn, if you can get them to admit their sins, your whole trip will be worth it." In the seminar, when I was ready to ask them to confess their sins aloud, I panicked at the possibility of nobody daring to pray. But God suddenly brought to my mind the words *all together*. After getting a whispered confirmation from my interpreter, I stood amazed as the whole room erupted in audible prayers—sounding like ten thousand swarming bees—women confessing their sins and asking God for forgiveness in front of each other. And they confessed their sins so fervently and so long that the interpreter finally asked them to stop so we could go on with the seminar. Prayer power— breaking the ice!

Then there was the thrill of seeing God overcome Satan's power in his incredible stronghold in South Taiwan. On the first night of the seminar, I felt almost as if there were chains binding me as I spoke. It took almost a whole night of wrestling in prayer by my missionary hostess and myself to bring victory over that evil power. But it broke and was gone, and God poured out His power on us all. We saw God vividly demonstrate the use of the last and often neglected piece of armor listed in Ephesians 6 with which to fight Satan—prayer (v. 18).

But this power in Taiwan was not the only result of the praying being done in America. God was answering prayers from both sides of the Pacific Ocean. Four women in Taiwan had been burdened for their island and were meeting regularly to pray. Then their number grew to thirty-five; and they prayed together for more than a year and, in faith, stepped out to invite me to come for prayer seminars there. These were the women God used to bring about the display of His power and the beginning of the binding together of the body of Christ in Taiwan.

God's power didn't stop working when I flew back to America either. The original group of thirty-five women in Taiwan has now been multiplied by Him to more than ten thousand praying women on this small island. It was God *"able* to do exceeding abundantly above all that we [could] ask or think" in answer to thousands of prayers.

I had called my mother from California to say good-bye

on my way to Taiwan. Her last words to me were: "Evelyn, don't forget Ephesians 3:20!" Mother, I shall never forget Ephesians 3:20!

Corporate Praying

Although there are many biblical promises of prayer power from one person's prayers, in Ephesians 3:20, the promise is addressed to many. It is plural—*"we* ask or think." And "according to the power that works in *us"* might well read "according to the amount of prayer for *us*—and by *us."*

In my thank-you letter to my pray-ers about God's power at work in my trip to Japan in 1981, I included these words: "I'm contemplating writing a book about the tangible evidences of *your prayers* in my life." This is the book! Who prayed? The secret of this power from God for ministry is corporate prayer with thousands of pray-ers releasing it.

Since 1968, we have been developing and practicing methods in my ministry of intercessory prayer that have produced His exceeding, abundant power. (See *What Happens When Women Pray.*[4]) And corporate prayer for serving the Lord has been an indispensable part of my life since 1964, when Signe, Lorna, and I started our four years of praying together every Thursday afternoon. This praying was the forerunner of the "What Happens When Women Pray" project of 1968, which has expanded around the world through our United Prayer Ministries, Inc. It has produced an astonishing series of lessons about what God is able to do when there is enough prayer. So prayer is not just a theory in my head of what should happen or might happen. I have seen it happen.

At the publisher's million-copy party for my book *What Happens When Women Pray,* I was asked to speak on the subject, "What produces a million-copy book?" My answer was simply, "Prayer." God literally produced the book. It was conceived in prayer, is about prayer, and was continuously prayed for through the writing, production, distribution, and its use—to this day.

But the book, published in 1975, was just another step in the prayer ministry God was able to open up because of prayer.

---

4. Evelyn Christenson, *What Happens When Women Pray* (Wheaton, Ill.: Victor Books, 1975).

After leaving our "What Happens When Women Pray" church in Rockford, Illinois, in 1970, God chided me to "stir up the gift . . . which is in [you]" (2 Tim. 1:6). Which gift? "Prayer! Start teaching what I taught you in all the prayer experimentation!" God replied.

These are the methods He taught us. **Just three**—Gloria Davidson, Jan Mudge, and I—started out. And we prayed through every step and every decision in our fledgling prayer seminar movement, knowing well that we didn't know how to do it, but we just had a tremendous burden to teach people to pray. We enlisted many faithful pray-ers to support us.

Then it was our praying about getting the seminar material on audio cassettes that led the three of us bravely to order one thousand sets from Bethany Fellowship, only to creep back like three timid mice to cut our order in half. Then we all prayed diligently and fervently that they would sell—which they did—immediately. In shock, I called Dave Anthony to tell him to put into production the other five hundred sets. I could almost feel him smiling over the phone as he answered, "I knew they would sell so I just went ahead and made the thousand sets. Just come out and pick them up."

Next came the praying for the book Victor Books asked me to write after hearing those tapes. In the meantime, we three had incorporated into United Prayer Ministries, Inc., praying through every unexplored step; and the board members had multiplied. It was my **Personal Telephone Prayer Chain** of about thirty women that upheld me during the writing of every word all those long months. For more than ten years, I have been sharing my physical, emotional, mental, and spiritual needs with this chain. And they have upheld me with their powerful prayers, sacrificially giving of their time and effort daily. Frequently, it was their deep striving and wrestling in prayer that enabled God to send forth our ministry.

Other corporate prayer, enabling God to produce that book and its subsequent ministry, came from my **Personal Prayer Group** of nine women, organized in 1971. How we agonized in prayer over each concept and word, titles, time in my schedule to work on it, guidance for those publishing it at Victor Books—and even a printers' strike! Also, the intercession for these needs by faculty wives at Bethel College and Seminary during our weekly prayer meetings—as well as by relatives, friends, and fellow church members—all corporately enabled God to release enough wisdom and power for that book on prayer.

But when I saw the first copy of *What Happens When Women Pray* and realized that I had promised to pray for each person reading the book, I panicked. How could I do that? So we devised a **Prayer Calendar** with each day assigned to an "intercessor," whose job it was to pray for those reading the book or teaching it that day (while the rest of us prayed for the intercessor). Now, more than ten years later, the calendar is still in operation, including daily prayer for everyone reading and teaching my books, those using the tapes, and my daily schedule.

I pass our experiences of answered prayer on to the interdenominational **Steering Committees** planning my seminar and request that they meet regularly for up to six months to pray. (They hardly need me after all of their unity and power in prayer!) But when I step into a seminar, I can feel the amount and quality of prayer that has been offered. God's power in my seminars is always directly proportional to the amount and kind of praying done by the committee.

Running Our Organization on Prayer

In our United Prayer Ministries (UPM), we depend completely on God's direction. When asking God for guidance, wisdom, or the opening of doors, we literally follow the advice in my first book—to "pray first and plan afterward." About half of each **Board Meeting** is actual praying. We usually open the meeting with an hour of prayer and then close with all taking part in extended praying, with prayer for present and future ministry after the business session. Then, while discussing business, we have found a fantastic secret for wisdom. When we do not know what decision to make, we just stop and pray. Between monthly board meetings, the praying continues with requests communicated through our UPM telephone prayer chains.

God taught us early that "prayer *is* the answer." And it has worked. We have no superstars, only "God's fellow-workers" (1 Cor. 3:9, NASB). Together with us, He has taken this prayer ministry around the world.

In addition to our own board telephone prayer chains, we organized an area-wide **Metropolitan Prayer Chain** in the Twin Cities of St. Paul and Minneapolis, consisting of several hundred members from all denominations. It has been the pilot project for similar ones in many countries around the world.

Our most active prayer chain is the **Government Telephone Prayer Chain,** praying for local, national, and world governments, leaders, and legislation. The participants research, pray diligently, and enlist further praying from other Christians.

Recently, after a debate that lasted past midnight, the full Minnesota Senate passed, by a preliminary vote of 32–27, a bill that gave state approval to a lifestyle which the Bible calls abhorrent to the Lord. Supporters expected certain victory at the final vote the next evening. However, Christians across the state went to prayer. Heavy phone responses caused five legislators to withdraw their support of the bill. Five others who had been absent during the preliminary vote also decided to oppose the measure. The bill's author knew it was futile to even present it again. He threw it on the floor and cursed "those Christians."

But success is not always visible and immediate. Someone once asked me, "Since there is all of this prayer, why is America's drug scene, abortions, pornography, child abuse, and so on getting worse?" My answer was, "What would America be by now if we hadn't had all that prayer?" I shudder to think!

Telephone prayer chains have no power in themselves, but they enable many people to pray simultaneously and immediately for a need without having to wait for mailed prayer lists or group prayer meetings.

Another use of the telephone for prayer is **Conference Calls.** I just hung up the phone after praying in a powerful prayer session with two others for revival in our nation's capital. Again, the time and effort spent in getting together physically is avoided, and the call is an effective "two or three together" method. A pastor in California told me he spends the first two hours of each day, starting at 5:00 A.M., in conference calls with his board members, prayer supporters, and even his mother-in-law!

The **Twenty-Four-Hour Prayer Clock** is one of the most powerful forces in our ministry. Operating only when I am overseas, it produces tremendous power for ministering along with my other pray-ers. Each person signs up for a specific period of time during which they promise to pray daily, along with the time of day or night they will pray, thus making an unbroken circle of intercession all the while I am gone.

This prayer clock usually stops praying for me when my plane touches down in Minneapolis-St. Paul. But when I returned from India in the fall of 1983, without telling me, they decided to add two days of prayer to get me through jet lag. After three weeks of an extremely intense schedule, excessive heat, intestinal problems, and conducting the whole National Prayer Assembly without my husband (who had flown home because of severe intestinal problems), I arrived home exhausted. To greet me were two new grandbabies and a son home from graduate school to celebrate his birthday. But, to my amazement, I had no jet lag. Kathy Grant, a twenty-four-hour prayer clock member from Washington, D.C., called me with a startling story: "Evelyn, as I prayed, I actually suffered *with* you in your jet lag."

"No, Kathy," I assured her, "you did not suffer *with* me, you suffered *for* me. I didn't have any jet lag!"

Feeling the Power

I learned quite by accident that feeling God's power is one of the experiences of people for whom we pray. Back in 1968, when we did our "What Happens When Women Pray" experimentation, I interviewed the people for whom we had prayed. Their most common response was, "Oh, I could *feel* you praying." What could they feel? The power of God released through prayer!

The president of the United States, Ronald Reagan, at the annual Presidential Prayer Breakfast after he had been shot, said to us, "Nancy and I want to thank you for praying. It is true that you can feel and sense that power!"

It was what our United Prayer Ministries board member, Dorothy, felt this weekend after receiving the shocking news that her only son had just been burned to death in Arizona. As I put my arms around her at the memorial service, I told her that we had been praying for her almost constantly. "I know," she said, smiling through her grief. "I could *feel* it. Thanks."

In Adelaide, Australia, when those five hundred out of a thousand women prayed aloud, making sure they knew Christ personally, I was so overwhelmed at feeling God's power in that room that I could not speak. I just stood there with tears streaming down my face. A large women's Bible study movement had invited me, and their international president had come down from the Philippines to attend the seminar. Afterward, she said, "When that happened it felt as if a surge of power ran down my back—almost like an electric shock."

Then the local president chimed in, "I felt the same thing. Did you feel it, Evelyn?"

"No," I replied, "I just stood there—unable to speak in the presence of that awesome power." Again, God was able to release His power because of all the prayer.

Power released through prayer was the difference Jeanne, our current board president, reported that she and her surgeon husband, Dr. Bill Scott, felt in Bangladesh. After finishing their missionary work in India, they returned to America where Bill was practicing surgery in a large Minneapolis hospital. Then they went to Bangladesh to complete a hospital in Parbatipur. After returning home, Jeanne told of the difference in what they *felt* from the prayer support of our board, our prayer chains, and other prayer-support groups. Of course, there had been fine missionary support the first time, but this time was different. She told me, "With the increased prayer support, God opened doors in remarkable ways, mobilizing resources and help so that in twenty months a hospital was dedicated and opened, as well as a chapel."

It was God's power released by corporate prayer that I felt in Central Hall, Westminster, London, where the first session of the General Assembly of the United Nations took place in 1946. As I mounted the huge marble staircase on the way to the speaker's platform, my back gave way due to a recurring lower back spasm, causing excruciating pain. But I was able to stand and speak all that day with God's strength literally being mine. Later, the president of the British Bible Society, learning of my almost unbelievable experience, said I must have sent word to my prayer chains back in America. "No," I answered, "they already were praying, and God knows my needs and how to answer." And He did!

On my first morning in Perth, Australia, last March, I wrote in my diary: "Feel great! No jet lag. Woke at 4:30 Perth time.

Lord, it's right on *the* dot! It was my usual waking time in America, but Australia is half-way around the world. This was in spite of fifty-three hours from my bed in St. Paul to the bed in Perth—caused by the second worst snowstorm in our history which hit Minnesota the day I was to leave, the airline going on strike just as I was to depart, and an eight-hour delay in Los Angeles. Then our pilot on Qantas Airlines quipped while we were still seeing only the Pacific Ocean below us that we were running out of gas (because of an unusually strong headwind), and we would be making an emergency landing in Brisbane. *"This is the strongest I've ever felt the pray-ers."* I underlined in amazement as I continued to write.

This morning in the predawn darkness while reviewing all the corporate prayer for me since 1964, my eyes suddenly filled with tears, tears of thanksgiving, as I realized the magnitude of all this combined prayer for me. My heart just exploded with thanks to God for the indescribable privilege of all those years of unbroken prayer support by so many.

I repeated in my mind the thanks I wrote to my pray-ers after I returned from the seminar series in England: "You also join in helping us through your prayers, that thanks may be given by many persons on our behalf for the favor bestowed upon us through *the prayers of many*" (2 Cor. 1:11, NASB, emphasis mine). And I, with Paul, "do not cease giving thanks for you, while making mention of you in *my* prayers" (Eph. 1:16, NASB, emphasis mine). At the beginning of my prayer ministry, our then high-schooler son, Kurt, said to me, "How can you miss, Mom, with all that prayer?" How very true, Kurt!

Above All That We Ask or Think

What Jeremiah said in the Old Testament of God showing us "things . . . thou knowest not" (Jer. 33:3), Paul said in the New Testament with his "above all that we ask or think" (Eph. 3:20).

No matter how much I expect from God, He always gives more. No matter how much faith I have, I never seem to have enough to equal the fabulous amount of whatever God is ready, willing, and anxious to do—when there is enough prayer. God's intention is to exceed by His answer even the far-reaching petitions of His pray-ers and the aspirations that prompted them.

While doing the first arm of "Mission: England" in 1983, one of my privileges was to sign up people for "triplets." In this method, three Christians each choose three people who do not know Christ and then promise to get together weekly to pray for those nine people until they find Christ as their Savior. Altogether, thirty thousand Christians signed up for the triplet groups prior to Billy Graham's six crusades comprising "Mission: England." These were in addition to the people in seventy-five countries who signed up to pray for his "Mission: England." And the outcome was phenomenal! Billy Graham reports that he had by far the greatest results in people finding Christ of any other crusade in his history. George Wilson, executive vice-president of the Billy Graham Evangelistic Association, excitedly reporting this to us, said, "And, Evelyn, we know why, don't we? It was all that prayer!" Yes, the prayers of all those dear people in England, who, in turn, had been prayed for by us as they signed up and prayed.

The Lausanne Committee for World Evangelization, sponsoring our first International Prayer Assembly in Seoul, Korea, in 1985, was anxious for us to emphasize Pentecost Sunday and scheduled the assembly to include this date. As head of the women's workshops, I had prayed repeatedly for six months, "Oh, God, send something of Pentecost to us at this Assembly." (Occasionally, while praying, I smilingly wondered, "if God would really decide to send some of what happened at Pentecost, how many of our international participants would flee for home? Were we really ready for that?")

The women's workshops met in the sanctuary of the Young Nak Church with simultaneous translators for each language being broadcast in booths. The people listened in their own language over their own radios with earphones; but, the first day, we did not have a Chinese translator along with the others. One of the reporters interviewing participants after each session was an American missionary who spoke fluent Chinese. Asking the Chinese delegation about the session, she was told how meaningful my lessons on the "cleansed life" and "forgiven as we forgive" and the praying afterward had been. "But," the reporter said, "you don't speak English."

"No," was their reply.

"And you didn't have a Chinese translator today," said the missionary.

"Oh," exclaimed the surprised Chinese women, "it must have been the Holy Spirit!"

I certainly had not asked for—nor even thought of—something that close to Pentecost, and I was reluctant to report it until I could validate it. But this had come from Faye Leung, the Chinese woman responsible for my Trans World Radio broadcasts into China, who also speaks fluent English. At dinner in Hong Kong after the Prayer Assembly, I asked Faye's opinion about it. She said, "Oh, that doesn't surprise me at all. I was praying that day with a Chinese woman who, although she doesn't understand a word of English, prayed each prayer you asked us to pray!" I'm sure the pray-ers before Pentecost hadn't asked or thought of what God had sent them either.

Exceeding Abundantly

I have not always expected most of the dramatic answers from God in this prayer ministry. When we started in 1968, I didn't even know if my church women would pray with me; and, if they did, if God would do anything. But now, with God's overwhelming responses, I know! But I also have become painfully aware of all the good things God desires to pour out on planet earth, which I limit Him from doing because I do not pray enough.

Over the crib for our grandbabies in our spare bedroom, I have hung a small needlepoint wallhanging. It says, "Prayer IS the answer!"

Dr. Paul Yonggi Cho, pastor of a now five hundred thousand-member church in Seoul, Korea, said to us while explaining the power for that kind of church growth, "Americans stay after church and eat. We stay after church and pray." I mentioned this at a recent pastors' conference. We then went to prayer, and one pastor blurted out, "Oh, God, I don't pray enough. Forgive my lack of prayer—my personal prayer, prayer with my family, prayer for my church. Oh, God, forgive me!" Surprisingly, almost no American seminaries teach for credit the subject of prayer and its power. But prayer is the key that unlocks God's omnipotent throne room.

In Ephesians 3:20, Paul gives us a tremendous look into God's mind. And I have found that life bathed in, saturated by, and directed through prayer, has been exhilarating and exciting. I feel as if I'm continuously standing on tiptoe, straining to peer into God's mind, wondering how and what He is going to do this time. Yes, I have learned about His "exceeding abundantly above all that [any of us could] ask or think" when we prayed.

Capable, yes. And able too—when there is enough prayer! How much power is God releasing because of *your* prayers? Then again, how much power is God waiting for you to unlock with your key of prayer?

Closing Prayer

Oh, God, I confess that there is not enough prayer in my life. Father, You are not able to do many of the things You desire to do here on earth because of my lack of praying. I long to see Your exceeding, abundant answers over and above anything I could ask or think. Lord, I commit myself to spend more time in prayer daily. Help me to discipline myself to more actual praying.

In Jesus' name, **Amen.**

3

You Prayed the Wrong Prayer

That God *will not* answer prayer under certain conditions is just as clearly taught in the Bible as is that He *will* answer the prayers of His children at other times. Even though they had prayed, James said: "Ye ask and do not receive, because ye ask amiss, to consume it upon your lusts" (see James 4:3).

There are two kinds of prayer to which God answers, "You prayed the wrong prayer." First, there is the prayer that asks for the wrong thing—which God in His holiness never would grant. But then, there is the prayer to which God would have answered yes, except that it was for the wrong reason.

Wrong Motives

The reason God sometimes answers no to our prayers is that we prayed with the wrong *motives.* Although the things for which we ask may be good in themselves, we want them for the wrong reasons. So, even though we do ask, we do not receive.

Motives are the *reasons* for praying as we do. The reason

for praying for a certain thing can in itself make it a "wrong prayer." What are wrong prayers? Those prayed to *"consume them upon our lusts."*

The word *lusts* in James 4:3 has been translated more recently as "pleasures," and accurately so. But to us today, the word *pleasures* basically means something that is good and positive. Then there are things that are good for Christians that also are translated "pleasures" in the Bible. However, this particular biblical word *pleasures* always is negative and off limits for Christians. The literal definition of the Greek word translated "pleasures" in James 4:3 is, "The gratification of natural desire or sinful desires." This word is much better understood today when translated "lusts."

The word, of course, is much broader in meaning than just sexual lusts. How shocking to realize that the prayers we ourselves are praying frequently are prayed with a wrong motive—to consume upon our lusts. And God must answer, "You prayed the wrong prayer."

Here are some of the common, everyday motives that creep into our praying: praise, fame, love of power, love of display, love of preeminence, status over others, ease, comfort, personal satisfaction, self-pleasing, self-vindication, gratification of sinful desires, and revenge.

While most of us are careful basically to pray for things we believe are good, and which God wants to grant us, we usually are completely unaware of the wrong motives that can be inspiring these prayers. And praying with wrong motives for things to which God usually answers yes spells failure in prayer.

For Whose Glory?

Wanting something for our own glory, not God's, is one reason why a prayer, although scripturally accurate and acceptable to God, is ruined by our reason for praying it.

I am astounded in my ministry at some of the motives that surface when people or groups are praying about having a prayer seminar. Several years ago, I had a severe leg problem and my doctor insisted that I miss a scheduled prayer seminar on the West Coast and stay in bed another week. But then at the end of that week, he decided I was well enough to travel, so I could conduct the seminar in a city near the one where the seminar had been canceled. I received a phone call from the very irate pastor of the church I missed; he was absolutely furious with me for not appearing in *his* church and then having all those people come to his competitor's church the next week.

I wondered what his reason really had been for wanting my seminar. Was it actually to teach people to pray? Was it really to bind the different churches together in unity? Or was it to attract people from all denominations of the area into *his* church? Was it basically to bring glory to *his* church—and to *him?* Although praying to have a seminar to teach people to pray certainly is a good prayer, the motive can be so wrong. And God answers, "You prayed the wrong prayer."

In 1979, as I prayed my birthday prayer for my life in the coming year, my words simply were these: "God, You be glorified, not me!" And when the year ended, my praying for only His glory did not end. Praying the "right prayer" about God getting all the glory has been a learning process for me for a long time.

Through the years, I have prayed before speaking that I will not be seen as I speak—only Jesus. After the sometimes flowery introduction is all over, I pray that what I am wearing, my hairdo, and so on will all fade from the audience's consciousness and be replaced by Jesus. The greatest compliment I ever receive is when someone steps up to me and quietly says, "I saw Jesus standing there instead of you all day today." For *His* glory!

Also, before a seminar, I always pray, "Lord, remove every illustration and point that will bring glory to me instead of You." The illustration or point may be very good in itself, but if my motive for bringing it is for *my* glory, God will not use it to move in the lives of those in my audience. It has to be for His glory.

We can even have the wrong motive in praying to win others to Christ. For whose glory do we want to bear spiritual fruit? Jesus in John 15:7–8 tells us that if we fulfill His conditions, we shall ask what we will and it shall be done unto us. But why? So that we can be glorified? Oh, no. It is so that we can bear much fruit—not for our glory but for the Father's. Are we trying to win another to Jesus to get credit ourselves or to swell the statistics of our church or organization? For whose glory?

A subtle motive of our receiving the glory instead of God

slips in when we have discovered something exciting and shared it with someone, only to have that person come out with it later in a discussion, in a sermon, or in a book! How it hurts when another gets the credit instead of we. But then we must examine the reason for feeling this way. God can get a lot done if we don't care who gets the credit—and the glory!

To Consume It on Our Lust of Pride

So many of our prayers are prayed with another wrong motive: *to be seen by people,* not God—so we will get the credit and glory. But Jesus, in Matthew 6:5, said our motive for praying is not to be as that of the hypocrites standing in the synagogues and on the street corners "in order to be seen by men" (NASB). This is a wrong motive; no matter how good the content of these prayers might be, the Lord is displeased.

This is the lust of display—one of the major reasons we ask and have not because we are asking to consume it upon this lust. How proud we can become by being known as "one who never skips prayer meeting" or "one who prays such beautiful prayers in public." Things good in themselves but done with the wrong motive. The lust of pride! God told Solomon that it was only when His people would *"humble themselves* and pray" that He would answer and "heal their land" (2 Chron. 7:14, NASB).

There also can be the motive of pride in our private devotional praying. I find that I must be constantly on the alert for wrong motives in my own prayer life, and usually, I am surprised when they surface.

While our Kurt was taking his entrance exams for a doctoral program in physics, I spent the three hours in prayer. Not knowing how to pray for three whole hours on the same subject, I asked God to teach me. One of the amazing things He showed me was that, although I sincerely was praying for God's will, some of my motives for wanting Kurt to pass those tests were wrong. It was God waving His yellow caution flag, "Watch it!"

Creeping into what I thought were only pure motives about God's will for my son's future was a wrong motive—pride.

I found myself praying a seemingly normal, motherly prayer: "Oh, God, what if Kurt's cousin Paul passes his tests and gets into his biomedical engineering program and our son flunks?" God's rebuke set me praying for forgiveness for the wrong motive in my praying.

Four years later, I found it much easier to heed God's yellow caution flag. I was deeply in prayer as Kurt feverishly wrote to get a report of a discovery of his published before a "competitor" in another university. He had been told inadvertently what Kurt was doing; and, if he published before Kurt, he would receive the credit for Kurt's discovery. As I prayed, I suddenly became aware that God was waving His caution flag. Immediately, I changed my prayer to, "Oh, God, You know who deserves to get the credit for this discovery. You know what Kurt's needs are—and also what he deserves."

In the whole section of James 4:1–3, one of the reasons for not receiving is that "you are envious" (v. 2, NASB). We always want immediate success, victory, and credit when praying for someone we love; but our motives can be to consume it upon our own lust—our pride.

James 4:6 tells us that "God is opposed to the proud" (NASB); so He certainly won't grant our requests that are prayed to be consumed on our lust of pride. A wrong motive makes it a wrong prayer—which, of course, God won't answer.

Your Kingdom, Not Mine

How many Christian leaders are building their own kingdoms, not God's? Here again, what they are praying for may be good and scriptural—a growing congregation, a larger church building, better headquarters for their organization or campus—but their *reason* for praying is for praise, fame, and glory for themselves.

But Jesus in His model prayer in Matthew 6, as He taught His followers to pray, was very explicit about whose kingdom must be built: "Our Father . . . *Thy* kingdom come . . . On earth as it is in heaven" (vv. 9, 10, NASB).

In a large, seemingly successful church in which I held a recent seminar, several members commented sadly to me, "But there is no power." Why? Perhaps it was because their very talented pastor might have been building not the kingdom of God and His glory but his own kingdom and his own reputation.

This love of preeminence, status over others, and building one's own kingdom instead of God's, seemed already to be a problem in the first century. In 3 John, the apostle John said that he needed to expose Diotrephes because he loved to be first among people. Diotrephes refused to acknowledge the apostle John, lest his own position of authority should be challenged.

We tend to think this wrong motive exists only in the large, splashy ministries; but, in actuality, it may be as true or even more true in the small, struggling churches and organizations. In a desperate attempt to prove their importance in a community or in their denomination, such churches resort to building their own kingdom instead of God's.

It is possible that we are deceiving ourselves, as well as other people, about our motives in prayer—but never God. He is aware of all our hidden attitudes and motives—many times unrecognized even by ourselves.

It is not only our words that ascend to God in prayer but our motives as well. God looks within—and our motives are just as obvious to Him as our spoken words. "And all the churches will know that I am He who searches the minds and hearts" (Rev. 2:23, NASB).

Praying with the wrong motive, then, is praying anything to which God must answer no because, although perhaps good in itself, the reason for praying is "to consume it upon our own lusts."

Asking Amiss

Praying with wrong motives actually is the cause of asking amiss which, of course, is praying wrong prayers.

We like to think that the "to ask amiss" of James 4:3 is just slightly missing the right content in our prayer. However, it means wicked, evil asking. To ask amiss literally means: "to ask evilly." It is praying for the satisfaction of those things that God explicitly calls on the true Christian to suppress. Thus, it is not a prayer that can be answered by God. A prayer that asks amiss must be answered by Him, "You prayed the wrong prayer."

But in John 15:7 (NASB), didn't Jesus promise that we could ask for *"whatever* [we] wish"? And then in this chapter's sixteenth verse, didn't He say that *"whatever* you ask of the Father in My name, He may give to you"? How, then, could anything we pray for be asking amiss and a "wrong prayer"?

Well, Jesus also gave us innumerable rules by which to live; and His promise for answers to our prayers did not, and could not, negate all His rules and commands. Jesus is truth (John 14:6). He cannot lie. How could He teach and demand purity, holiness, and righteousness and then imply in His prayer promises that we could ask for—and receive—just the opposite?

Again, Jesus said in John 14:14, "If you ask Me *anything* in My name, I will do it" (NASB)—seemingly giving us a blank check to request any amount of anything we choose. However, in His preceding words, He clearly says why He will do whatever we ask in His name—"that the Father may be glorified in the Son" (John 14:13, NASB)! So, obviously, Jesus would never promise anything in answer to prayer that would not glorify the Father. And certainly, those things that God calls on us to suppress because they are sin would not be granted— even if prayed "in the name of Jesus."

No—all of our prayers must conform to and adhere to God's rules and laws as set forth for us in the Bible. They must be based on scriptural guidelines. They must be in the confines of God's will as set forth in Scripture. Proverbs 28:9 actually says, "He that turneth away his ear from hearing the law [literally, the Word of God], *even his prayer shall be abomination."*

A young wife and mother kept calling me from Hawaii about her husband and his girlfriend. One day, she asked, "Is it all right for me to ask God, if it is His will, to allow my husband to leave me and marry her, because God wants him to be happy?"

"No," I retorted, "don't ever pray that prayer. God's answer to that prayer already is in the Bible. God explicitly said that it is not His will for a marriage to break up." I explained to her that, in Matthew 19:6, God clearly said, "Consequently they are no more two, but one flesh. What therefore God has joined together, let no man separate" (NASB). Then I told her God's words in Malachi 2:16 as He almost thundered, "I hate divorce" (NASB). You do not pray for the fulfillment of your husband's sexual lusts—but for him to suppress them.

Resentment and refusal to submit ourselves to any kind of scripturally required restraint is sin. And praying for things in opposition to what God's Word teaches certainly is "wrong praying."

Here, again, the word *pleasures* in James 4:3 is the same word Jesus used in the parable of the soils in Luke 8:14: "The seed which fell among the thorns, . . . are choked with worries and riches and *pleasures* of this life, and bring no fruit to maturity" (NASB). Writing to Titus, Paul used the same word, "For we also once were foolish ourselves, disobedient, deceived, enslaved to various lusts and *pleasures*" (Titus 3:3, NASB). So asking for something that would choke and enslave us certainly is praying "wrong prayers."

Peter put it this way: "Beloved, I urge you as aliens and strangers to abstain from fleshly lusts, which wage war against the soul" (1 Pet. 2:11, NASB). Our bodies and minds are the camping ground and battlefield of these lusts. So, how could God grant us our wishes when those things for which we pray wage spiritual war within us? Praying for them is gross "asking amiss."

The history of Christendom reveals many parallels of asking for God's blessing on something evil—slave-traders piously asking God's blessing on their wicked traffic, and Italian outlaws propitiating their patron saint before attacking bands of travelers. Today, how many of us piously lift our voices to the holy God of heaven and then ask for something He calls an abomination?

God never promised, "Delight yourself in your neighbor's wife, and I will give you the desires of your heart." No! The Psalmist told us God's way: "Delight yourself *in the Lord;* and He will give you the desires of your heart" (Ps. 37:4, NASB).

God rebukes us for delighting in the wrong thing. But Paul gives us an example of praying "the right prayer" in his prayer for those in the church at Thessalonica. "To this end also we pray for you always that our God may count you worthy of your calling, *and fulfill every desire for goodness and the work of faith with power;* in order that the name of our Lord Jesus may be glorified in you, and you in Him, according to the grace of our God and the Lord Jesus Christ" (2 Thess. 1:11–12, NASB, emphasis mine).

Every prayer, in order to be the "right prayer" which can be answered by God, must pass the test of His omniscience, His sovereignty, and His holiness.

Good—But Still Wrong—Prayers

There are many other prayers to which God must also answer, "You prayed the wrong prayer." They are not evil in themselves at all or even petitioned with a wrong motive. In fact, they are just the opposite. The pray-er may be sincerely seeking to do what is scriptural and what seems to be God's will. To these pray-ers, God *lovingly* must say, "You prayed the wrong prayer." It seems as if He kindly is saying, "Thanks anyway, but. . . ."

" 'For My thoughts are not your thoughts, neither are your ways My ways,' declares the LORD. For *as* the heavens are higher than the earth, So are My ways higher than your ways, And My thoughts than your thoughts" (Isa. 55:8–9, NASB). These are not evil prayers—but God knows something we don't.

You Are Not Ready Yet

God tenderly must explain to us at times that "your timing is not My timing." In our zeal, we often get ahead of God's timing for us. Not that the prayer in itself isn't good—it just may not be for us at that time. This response from God to prayer, of course, seems like a no answer. And God may or may not explain at the time that it is just a "Wait, I have more to do *in* you before I can answer yes."

This answer to my call to foreign missions at the end of our schooling was an especially hard one for me to handle. After I had prayed, submitting my whole life to God's will, I was sure God was giving this call—to which I had answered in prayer a deep, final yes. But then I thought God had decisively slammed shut the door to foreign missions once and for all.

I was absolutely devastated when our denomination's Foreign Mission Board's examining doctor decided that Chris's war-related ulcers would not allow him to serve where finding milk and cream could be a problem—the standard treatment for ulcers in those days. At the next foreign missions commissioning service, I sobbed as all the others were sent off—except us. In fact, for several years, I avoided that part of our denomination's annual meeting, for I could not face the hurt and bitterness in my soul when God's call to India had seemed so definite.

Chris had been a World War II bomber pilot and, in a burning B-17 plane over Germany, had promised God that if He would bring him safely to neutral territory he would serve Him the rest of his life. He even instructed pilots in the early Missionary Aviation Fellowship program. Then at the end of the preparation years at college and seminary, together we accepted God's call to foreign missions in Assam, India. Chris was to be the first flying evangelist in that country, and we were ecstatic.

However, being the secretary to our college president for four years hardly had prepared me for the mission field. Even the difficult war years, three miscarriages, and other family tragedies hardly had either. And certainly, a liberal arts college education hadn't done all that much. But nobody had seemed very concerned about what I would do once I got there. So I was as excited and committed as any missionary candidate could be.

But God's door to India for us stayed tightly shut for thirty whole years. However, God's answer really was not no but just His *"I have much preparing to do in you."* And the steps of preparation have been long and slow. But in 1982, Chris and I finally went to India.

As I was speaking for the first time in New Delhi, I was so choked up that I could hardly speak. Tears kept filling my eyes as I told these women of my devastating disappointment in 1952—and now my overwhelming joy thirty years later.

Our omniscient God has reasons for His timing in fulfilling calls. I'm sure He knew I was not ready to go to India in 1952. But these thirty years have prepared me through eighteen years in my husband's pastorates, the "What Happens When Women Pray" experimenting, my books, tapes, and the privilege of personally training hundreds of thousands to pray in seminars in the United States and Canada and overseas.

As we did leave for India, included in the Scripture our Jan gave us were these words about God's sovereign timing from Psalm 31:15, *"My times are in thy hand."*

In our impatience, we try to tell God *when* we want our prayers answered. But how good God is to control the timing of His answers to our prayers. However, our prayers do start a process in our lives that prepares us for the answer—only to emerge years later as the answer to what we desired so long before.

Is the World Ready?

It is also possible that God knows that not only are we not ready, but the world is not yet ready for what He has called us to do. For years before the printing of my book *What Happens When Women Pray,* people at my prayer retreats and seminars would say that they thought the ideas about what produces power in prayer should be in print. "If you think so," I would always answer, "then you pray about it."

But when God did say almost miraculously, "Write it!" I realized that something new was happening in our country. There was a turning of Christians to a dependence on God not known for many years. We had been an "I can do it myself, God" generation. But Watergate had humbled us, and we became "the ugly Americans" in many places overseas. Christians were ready and, yes, eager to learn more about prayer. I believe that had the book been published sooner it would not have sold as many copies. But when it did come out, people were ready to pray. God's timing, not mine!

I have learned that God's timing is not my timing in the big and little things about which I pray. Sometimes God keeps me persisting in prayer, becoming more fervent in my wrestling with Him, through days, months, and even years. And then there are times when I know He is directing me to release the request back to Him after praying, and I just wait for His answer to come—when He decides it is time to send it.

But He always answers. In my life, there are what I call "answer times," which come suddenly—when God knows it is time, and multiple answers just start flowing. And I struggle to grasp them all, like feverishly plucking dandelion seeds scattering in the wind.

You Are Not Spiritually Ready to Handle That

God is too loving to answer our prayers before we are spiritually mature enough to handle them. Many times, He must withhold the answers He wants to give us because He knows we have not matured enough spiritually. Then, He answers our prayer with "I love you too much to give you that."

Our Jan had six-hour microsurgery at the Mayo Clinic to enable her to become pregnant with her first child, our little granddaughter, Jennifer. Last fall, Jan and Skip felt God was telling them it was time to have another child; but tests showed the surgery would have to be repeated if there was to be any chance of pregnancy. Jan was more than willing, but we all shuddered at such a high price to pay for little ones.

So, for months, we literally bombarded heaven with a barrage of prayers for God to perform a miracle. There was no lack of faith that the God who created Jan could perform what was humanly impossible—but so simple for Him. As the time drew near for her last date to become pregnant before the scheduled surgery, I felt almost a little tingly in my whole being as I was anticipating God's answer.

But then I questioned whether my attitude might not be from God at all and earnestly sought His face. Suddenly, I admitted to myself that I was not in condition spiritually for what He might answer. If the last chance for Jan to become pregnant passed, how disappointed would I be? Could I handle it? Was it really God speaking? If not, who? "Oh, God," I cried, "prepare *me* for Your answer!"

Then I wondered, "What if He does answer by giving a baby without surgery?" How would I handle that? Would I remember all the prayer? Would I be able to give *Him* all the glory? What would I become if I received the answer I wanted? Would it do me harm? "Lord, *am I ready* for Your answer? Oh, God, prepare *me!*"

Then came the phone call from Jan that her last possible test before surgery was negative. I cried. "Lord, which one, or ones, of us was not prepared for Your miracle? Was it I? Which one of us would not have given You all the glory? Which one would have thought it was *our* power in prayer rather than *Your* power in answering? Which one would have become arrogant or prideful at our special place in Your plans? Which one, or ones, of us did not deserve a miracle? All of us?"

The motive of spiritual superiority is a lust covered in James 4:3. What would we have done with a miraculous answer of "no surgery necessary for this pregnancy"? And what would it have done to us?

God will never bestow upon us anything above our capacity to receive and exercise, even when we ask in prayer. He will do as much *for* us and *through* us as we have let Him do *in* us.

Alone in the house after Jan's call, I spent most of the day in contemplative prayer. "My God, my heart is weeping—and so are my eyes. Oh, God, prepare me for Your answers to all my prayers that You are just waiting to give!"

In a letter from Tasmania, Australia, a Christian woman wrote, "I had to go to hospital for an operation. I had prayer for healing a month before that, but the operation was still necessary. I can now see why. The Lord had a lot to teach me, the first thing being trust—and it had to be complete trust. The next thing was joy in my circumstances. While I was in hospital, the Lord gave me peace and joy and many prayers to pray for others in my ward—and then to see those prayers answered in front of my own eyes!"

No, God's love will never bestow anything on us above our spiritual capacity to handle it—even when we ask in prayer.

"My Purpose, Not Yours"

There are also times when God must answer, "You prayed the wrong prayer," because His purpose for our lives is not the same as ours might be—even though our purpose in itself may not be wrong.

In Bristol, England, in May 1983, God had to jog my memory that my feelings and the purpose for which He had called me might not be the same. My husband had become ill the first days of my "Mission: England" seminar tour in the British Isles. The day after he left to return to America, I did some deep heart-searching in prayer about completing that five-week mission.

From the time I was twenty-three years of age, my philosophy of life had been based on Romans 8:28 that "all things work together for good to them that love God, to them who are the called according to *his* purpose."

I struggled long in agonizing prayer for an answer. True, Chris had returned to the home of our daughter, Jan, and her husband, both physicians; and our other daughter and Chris's brother, also a doctor, were in the same city. But what was my first responsibility—as a wife or as a servant of God? I felt as if I was being torn in two parts, half of me longing to go home with him—and the other half facing my responsibility to the thousands who had signed up for seminars in the first arm of "Mission: England."

Then God gently directed me back to my Romans 8:28, and I turned to read it once again in my Bible. But this time, God's emphasis was not on the usual, "all things" or "good" or "who love him," but was reinforcing that He had called me "according to *his* purpose," not mine.

Since 1968, my "Lord, change me" prayer has been, "Lord, make me the *wife* You want me to be." And through the years, I have tried to live this prayer. But as I agonized over it once again, God gently changed the emphasis to a different word. It then was, "Lord, make me the wife *You* want me to be."

His purpose? Tossing to and fro with the wind as the circumstances fluctuate? Oh, no. God always had known what His purpose would be for me for different times of my life. As the writer of the Book of Hebrews explained in 6:17, "the unchangeableness of His purpose" (NASB).

Our deep prayer of submission is always what God expects when He has called us "according to his purpose." While I was reading Galatians 5 in a "Lord, Change Me" seminar in Stockton, California, God stopped me at verse 17, "For the flesh sets its desire against the Spirit, and the Spirit against the flesh; for these are in opposition to one another, so that you may not do the things that *you* please" (NASB, emphasis mine).

After reading this, my submission prayer to God, the Author of these words, was, "Lord, I see that I cannot do the things that *I* please. Whatever the next steps are, they are Your decision, not mine." "Lord," I continued praying, "I submit to *all* You please! I do not hold back because of a chance of being misunderstood. I want what You want only. No more. But, oh, God, *no less.* I love You, Lord!"

Jeremiah said it so well in 29:11, " 'For I know the plans that *I* have for you," declares the LORD, 'plans for welfare and not for calamity to give you a future and a hope' "

(NASB). His purpose, not mine! And I stayed to complete my mission.

"That Is Not for You"

At times, we may pray for something good and even scriptural that God has decided is not for us. For other people perhaps—but not for us. And our persistence in this prayer does no good for this can be one of God's "you prayed the wrong prayer" answers.

While in my thirties, I prayed repeatedly for the "gift of administration," which, of course, is one of the gifts mentioned in 1 Corinthians 12:28 in the list of spiritual gifts. I had watched my husband's secretary, Carolyn Carlson, with her tremendous gift of administration and longed for it too. I kept thinking of all the wonderful things I could organize for God— if He just would give me the gift of administration.

So I begged and pleaded with God to give me this gift. But this was the wrong prayer—and God never gave me the gift of administration. However, it was not until I finally realized that God withholds gifts just as deliberately as He gives them that I realized He knew what He was doing, and I accepted His no answer.

But this was not God being mean and withholding a good, scriptural gift. It was God answering me that He had called me "according to his purpose" and not according to what I thought I should be and do. God knew that I would have just twenty-four hours each day, and He had decided before the foundation of the world how He wanted me to spend them. I had been praying the wrong prayer.

I still occasionally wish I had that wonderful gift; but God's plan for me from the beginning was that I should study and teach, not spend time organizing everybody and everything.

So, praying for a gift God absolutely did not intend for me to have was spending all that time praying the wrong prayer. And through the years, He graciously has provided my Sally, whose gift *is* that wonderful gift of administration, to run my ministry—while I do those things He *did* equip me to do.

"Not for Them Either"

Another time God answers "that is not for you" is when He firmly and with finality says, "That is not for you—but only for My children." Without having accepted Christ, many people are praying for the things God has promised only to His children. If people do not know Christ as Savior and Lord, there is no promise in the New Testament that God will grant them their wishes.

The promises of God's peace, that He will work all things together for their good, and give His direction in their lives— and His joy, strength, and grace—are not mentioned any place in the Bible as being for those outside the body of Christ. God did not give these promises to those who have rejected His Son, Jesus, and thus do not have Him as their Savior and Lord.

"My Will, Not Yours"

Sometimes, we try to thwart God's will by the prayers we pray. But God then answers, "You are praying the wrong prayer." We must never forget that God is sovereign.

A pastor's wife told me that her husband was so enamored with his mistress (a woman in their church) that he always walked the long way to and from church just to walk by her house. Living in this sin and guilt, he was on the verge of an emotional collapse. But his wife told me she was trying to protect him from God's wrath and was continually praying: "Oh, God, he's so close to a nervous breakdown—don't convict him of his sin. He won't be able to handle it. He'll collapse emotionally."

"What a desperately wrong prayer to pray," I told her. "The only hope for your husband is for God to show him that what he is doing is a grievous sin—and then to so convict him that he will repent, straighten out, and turn from his wicked ways."

God's will is never to coddle a sinner and just ignore the sin because we ask Him to. No, this is praying strictly against His will—and praying the wrong prayer.

Then there are those times when what we are praying for really is God's will too; but His overriding rule is that He has given each person on earth a free will and will not coerce them. Woo them—yes. Coerce them—no.

A wife, whose husband had abandoned her, had asked God to send him back home by Christmas. But she called the day after Christmas and just yelled over the phone at me, "I'm so angry at God! I even screamed at Him. I just asked Him to send my husband home by Christmas. All I wanted was one little miracle." Spewing out her venomous feelings, she shouted, "I just told God I hated Him because He is capable of performing this miracle and bringing my husband back—but He didn't! God is able to do it—but He won't!"

"Don't be angry with God," I replied. "Of course, He is able. But God also has given everyone, including your husband, a free will. God's will is definitely for your husband to come back to his family. Your husband knows that is right, too; but if he absolutely refuses to do it, God still will allow him his freedom of choice.

"But," I assured her, "God will woo and work on your husband in proportion to your praying. However, don't blame God for your husband's rebellion. That is praying the wrong prayer."

When another woman shared her story with me at a weekend "Lord, Change Me" retreat, I questioned whether her praying "to be single and serve the Lord full time" was a right prayer. "I came here today to get out of the house. I've been married eighteen years to an unsaved, unfaithful, critical husband whom I'm in the process of planning to divorce," she said.

"My sixteen-year-old daughter has run away five times and has torn our family apart. She's done drugs since the sixth grade," she continued. "I have a thirteen-year-old girl and a five-year-old girl. I'm thirty-nine, have been saved since age seven, and have been a good, godly wife and mother. I want to be single and serve the Lord full time. I know God will guide and direct me. Please pray for me."

Where did God really want her to "serve Him full time"? What was His will about her being a mother to those children—all three of them? I asked her if she had considered these aspects. Her no answer made me see—she had been praying the wrong prayer.

We must be careful not to pray these wrong prayers, for the outcome may not be as great as we expected it to be. The Bible tells us that God sometimes actually will give us our request, but it will not be with His blessing—but with His judgment. When the children of Israel left Egypt and journeyed to the Promised Land, Psalm 106:14–15 tells us that they "lusted exceedingly in the wilderness, and tempted God in the desert. And he gave them their request; but sent leanness into their soul."

But at the same retreat, a young, abused wife for whom we had been praying in our prayer chains in Minnesota told me a different story. "My husband who has been abusing me has now left our child and me—and I don't want him back. It's so much better this way!"

Of course, God's will is for these marriage partners to be reunited. But only He knows if her prayers that he not come back—at least not until he changes his lifestyle—are wrong.

However, there is one prayer that never is "the wrong prayer." When we pray what Jesus taught us to pray in His model Lord's Prayer, it always is the "right prayer." And this prayer is, "Our Father. . . . *Thy* will be done" (Matt. 6:9–10).

How can we be sure we are not "praying the wrong prayer"? First, we must stay in the Bible to become aware of what is right and what is wrong in God's eyes. This will enable us to identify those prayer requests that are innately evil in themselves. Then, after praying a request, we wait in God's presence letting Him examine our motives for praying what we did. And God will bring these wrong motives to our minds and guard us from praying "wrong prayers."

Then God never will have to rebuke us with "You prayed the wrong prayer!"

Closing Prayer

Dear Father, show me the wrong prayers I have been praying. Please forgive me for not reading the Bible enough to find Your right things for which I ought to pray. And please search my heart for my wrong motives in even the good things I pray for. Cleanse me, O God, from all evil desires.

In Jesus' name, **Amen.**

4

WHEN GOD ANSWERS . . .

I Prerecorded That Answer

God frequently answers our prayer inquiries with "I already told you that." Then He adds, "I prerecorded that answer for you!" How? Where? In the Bible. God has prerecorded in His holy Word most of the instructions we will ever need in our whole lifetime. Then He leads us to them in direct answer to our prayers.

This is an amazing procedure in which God does not give the answer during our prayer, as He frequently does, but rather leads us to the Scripture that contains the answer to our request. When we pray, asking Him for something specific, He replies with a specific prerecorded answer from the Bible.

God communicates with us through the Bible in many different ways. While reading or studying His Word we may or may not know our need, but God does. And He takes the initiative to rebuke, comfort, or instruct us as we are reading. However, this method is different. Being acutely aware of a need or some instruction, we seek His answer in prayer, then God brings to our minds the place where He already has recorded the answer in the Bible.

The Author Is Always Present

Why can we get specific answers from a book whose closing words were written almost two thousand years ago? Because the Bible is the only book on planet earth where the Author is always present while it is being read.

I am continuously surprised at people's reaction to having the actual author of a book in their midst. Some stand in awe, wondering if they might touch us, while others question if we are really human. Yet, the very God of the universe is present with us every time we read His book. But how few of us treat the Bible that way! How little awe or excitement we display at having its Author, the very God of heaven, actually speaking to us about our personal needs and desires. In fact, many people seem to ignore Him completely while reading and studying the Bible.

Ways God Answers from the Bible

How does God answer us by His Word? There are four basic ways. Sometimes when I've been asking God in prayer for an answer, He just shows me in the portion of Scripture I'm currently reading devotionally. Then there are times when He brings to mind a thought or word that will be a clue as to where I should look. Occasionally, He will remind me of a book of the Bible or a chapter or a place on a page where He has my answer. And, occasionally, I'm startled to find the answer staring at me from the page to which I have randomly turned. Let me illustrate ways in which He has answered from the Bible.

1. It was the night before my first prayer seminar in Japan when *God used where I was reading devotionally* to influence not only me but all my audiences throughout the Japanese prayer seminar tour.

Chiko Templeman was dedicated, winsome, and beautiful and seemed to be the ideal interpreter for me on this tour. She was an excellent Bible study teacher in Washington, D.C., and had taught my prayer material in Japanese several times. After Chiko and her church raised her expenses, she joined me in Tokyo.

But I suddenly found myself almost panicking the night before my first seminar. Doubts overwhelmed me. Twenty years had passed since Chiko had married an American soldier and moved to the United States. I fretted, "Has the Japanese language so changed in that period of time to make the understanding of her interpreting difficult?" Even worse, I had just been told that the Japanese language was spoken differently in three levels of their society. I agonized, "As the granddaughter of a former prime minister of Japan, does she speak only that exclusive formal Japanese which will make our audiences uncomfortable or even unable to grasp what she is saying?"

Almost trembling physically at the thought of being unable to communicate with our Japanese audience, I prayed desperately. I felt as if I were actually shaking on the inside as I begged God for an answer.

Picking up my Bible, I turned to where I was reading devotionally, ready to start Psalm 16. And there it was—verse 8: "Because He is at my right hand, I *will not be shaken!*" (NASB). I relaxed in God's answer. The Psalmist's confidence in God became mine.

The next morning as I stood before a huge Japanese audience with Chiko at my left side, I opened with, "You can see only two people on this platform, but actually there are three. Last night, the God of the universe promised me that He would be on my right hand. You cannot see Him, because He is Spirit. But He is here. And He will tell me what to say to you. I will say it in English, then Chiko will say it to you in Japanese." Their response was overwhelming. We were communicating! And never once did we lose rapport that day—or throughout the five-week tour.

At our farewell, our missionary hosts asked how I ever understood the Oriental mind like that. I explained that I really had not. It was God's prerecorded answer in Psalm 16:8 that did it when He said that, because He was at my right hand, I should not be shaken.

2. Then there are those times when *God brings words to my mind that direct me to His answer.* However, this method necessitates having spent time in the Bible. Unlike reading devotionally until He speaks, which requires no previous knowledge of the Bible, God can only bring Scriptures to

our minds with which we are already acquainted. And the better we know the Bible, the more He can direct us to it for answers.

I learned this lesson vividly in Taiwan. As we flew to southern Taiwan to our second prayer seminar series, I was warned that this was one of Satan's most powerful strongholds in the world. Spirit worship was everywhere. Shrines dotted the fields and were even in the homes of the Christian wives attending our seminar who had pagan husbands. Evil seemed to permeate the very air we breathed. I felt I could almost reach out and touch it.

A great spirit of oppression was on my body and my mind as I spoke the first night. Back in my room, I struggled in prayer for many, many hours. My missionary hostess, who was used to such spiritual battles, fasted and prayed most of the night.

Early the next morning, I implored God for the Scripture that would break this oppression. All He brought to my mind were two words: *Psalms* and *delight.* And *delight* to me meant Psalm 37:4. So I turned to it and read it once again, "Fret not yourself because of evildoers, . . . Delight yourself in the Lord; and He will give you the desires of your heart" (Ps. 37:1, 4, NASB).

"Oh, Lord," I prayed, "my *desire* is that You would break this oppression and pour out Your power on this prayer seminar and on those dear ones living in the midst of this awful oppression of the enemy, Satan." Then I read verse 5, and I had God's method. First, "Commit your way to the LORD." This I had done thoroughly when coming all alone to Taiwan, never having even met anyone from there. Second, "Trust also in Him." "Oh, God," I cried, "I am trusting this morning. You know I am." Then, third—His answer, "And He will do it" (Ps. 37:5, NASB).

I claimed the victory. I recorded in the margin of my Bible, "This morning great power in prayer!!" I thanked Him and praised Him as I prayed. *He* was going to do it. I threw on my robe and, beaming, dashed across the hall to my missionary hostess, and exploded, "It's OK. The victory is here!"

My hostess rose from her knees, her eyes shining. "I know, I know," she exclaimed. God had just given her the *same Scripture*—with the same answer. *He* had broken the oppression. Together, we shed tears of joy, rejoicing over what God was going to do that day—which He did! From that time on, there was not one moment of oppression or lack of great power sweeping through our "What Happens When Women Pray" seminar!

In the times when you do not have within yourself the power to do something God has given you to do, have you learned that His wonderful prerecorded answer is already available to you?

3. *Bringing to my mind a book of the Bible, a chapter, a verse, or a place on the page,* once in a while, God gives me His prerecorded answer. This is not an everyday experience, but it happens occasionally when I am deeply in prayer, asking God for an answer.

One such instance occurred right after the Presidential Prayer Breakfast on January 31, 1985, in Washington, D.C. I was exhausted from a strenuous schedule, including Prison Fellowship's board meeting and an annual international banquet the night before, and rising for that breakfast with only a few hours of sleep. After the breakfast, I crawled back into my bed at the Washington Hilton, telling myself I deserved to spend time alone in prayer with the Lord for, after all, it was my birthday!

I always wait on the Lord for His specific birthday prayer for me for the coming year, so I lifted my heart to Him and said, "God, I really need something for *myself* for this year." I continued praying, "I'm exhausted from digging up all the old hurts to write them in this book. It's bad enough to experience them once, but to live through them over and over to get them written in a book is so hard. Lord, I'm drained emotionally and physically."

Immediately, God brought to my mind the lower left-hand page in my Bible. Then the word *Psalms* and the number 4 came to my mind. I picked up my Bible, and there it was— Psalm 4—starting on the lower left side of the page.

As I read the Psalm, there were many promises; but nothing specific came. Then I read it once again, and there it was: Psalm 4:7a. It almost jumped off the page at me. "Thou hast put gladness in my heart." I wrote in my Bible, "Amazing certainty! I felt the heaviness melt away—replaced with actual gladness."

Then I became aware of a big grin on my face and was surprised by a spontaneous, audible laugh. The gladness was there—replacing the misery. And God had given me my 1985 birthday prayer, which He had prepared and prerecorded for me from before the foundation of the world—and presented it to me on my birthday!

4. Then there are those very rare instances where His prerecorded answer is *on the page of the Bible to which I randomly turn.*

It was our daughter Jan's due date for her second baby, and I had been praying for an hour and a half that morning at the cottage about the delivery of her baby. Extensive microsurgery had been required once again to make conception possible, so this day was especially important to all of us. I prayed, claiming the blood of Jesus against Satan in the possibility of the cord around the baby's neck, lack of oxygen to the brain, our daughter's body, and so on. Then I asked God for the peace and assurance I needed at this critical time.

After praying, I decided to look up a verse of Scripture I needed for the section I was working on in the writing of this book. But as I picked up my Bible and opened it, my eyes immediately fell on a verse. There was no scanning or searching for something appropriate. In fact, I was actually looking for something completely different. But the verse on which my eyes fell was an incredible answer to my morning's prayer. Psalm 22:9, "Yet Thou art He who didst bring me forth from the womb" (NASB).

The thought engulfed me. God's hands would be lifting that little one from the womb to breathe the air of that birthing room. It would be His omnipotent hands, not just the doctor's, that would securely hold that tiny body. It was His sovereign will that would decide on every bit of timing and condition of mother and baby! My heart soared at the security I felt. The assurance!

God had the answer there for me all along, but He had waited to give it to me when I needed it specifically that morning. Also, God guided my thumbs as I opened my Bible. God directed my eyes to fall on that uniquely appropriate verse. God directed my heart to Him instead of the possible problems in that birth. And God lifted my apprehension and turned it into a granitelike faith in Him—with His prerecorded answer to my prayer.

Two weeks later, this same answer also kept me serene and trusting when Jan, with us watching the delivery, suddenly lost one-half of her blood. The peace never left. God was in control, engulfing us with His presence in that birthing room at the hospital.

We read in 1 Samuel 3:1 that, when the boy Samuel was ministering to the Lord before Eli, "word from the LORD was rare in those days" (NASB). But today we do not live in a period of such leanness. We have the Word of the Lord all prerecorded and waiting for us to seek answers from it.

Different Tones of Voice

Sometimes, I can almost hear the different tones in God's voice when He gives us His prerecorded answers. He doesn't chant in the monotone with which we tend to read the Scripture. Sometimes, He uses a chiding tone with us for not remembering what He has already told us or a scolding tone when we ask, but already know His answer. Then sometimes, it seems as though He sighs in relief that we have finally asked. Here are some of the many kinds of responses God uses in answering the questions we ask in our prayers.

"Don't insult Me," God declares in an indignant voice when we whine, "God, is it all right if I do so and so?" "Is it all right if I don't forgive so and so after what they did?" "Father, is it OK if I tell it this way? You know it's just a little white lie." "Could I have just a 'little friendly time' with him or her?" "Is it permissible for me to spend just this one little check without reporting it for taxes?"

Outraged, God answers, "If you have to ask *if,* you already know My answer. Don't insult Me by asking!"

Hebrews 1:1, 2 tells us that God had communicated with us in two ways—through the prophets of long ago and then through the manifestation of His Son, Jesus. But since Jesus returned to heaven at His ascension, how does the Father now communicate with us? One way is by answering our prayers. And a large percentage of these answers were recorded by "holy men of God" (2 Pet. 1:21) for us in the Bible.

So, let us not insult God by asking again when we already know what He has prerecorded for us. These are prayers we do not pray because He already has answered them for us in the Bible.

"I already told you that," God impatiently reminds us when

He has prerecorded specific instructions about the matter we are questioning.

People frequently question me about asking God if it is His will that they pray for the salvation of another person. God must sigh patiently—or more likely, impatiently—at these prayers as He leads them once again to His prerecorded will in 2 Peter 3:9, telling them that He is not willing for *any* to perish. Or to 1 Timothy 2:1–4 where He tells us that praying for others is good and acceptable in His sight, because He desires *all* to be saved. So His prerecorded answer once again is "I already told you that."

But they also ask another question of God, "God, since it is Your will that none should perish, why don't You answer my prayer and make them accept Christ?" And God replies that He also has a law that He will not break—that every person has been given a free will. He will not allow any person to usurp the inalienable right of every human being—the right of free choice. Otherwise, Jesus would have declared that every inhabitant in Jerusalem had to be saved; but instead, He wept over them, wanting to gather them as a hen gathers her chicks, but they were unwilling (Matt. 23:37).

"So the reason you should pray for them," God replies, "is that I will woo them and move in their lives in proportion to your prayers." It is not enough just to desire the salvation of the lost. Paul not only desired that the lost be saved but prayed to that end, "Brethren, my heart's desire and my prayer to God for them is for *their* salvation" (Rom. 10:1, NASB).

"Don't blame Me," God frequently retorts when things go wrong in our lives.

I was reading some Scripture passages in Galatians with a person who had sinned grievously in a sexual way and was struggling to work through confessing it. Suddenly, a question burst forth in prayer, "God, are You punishing me?" Together, we read God's prerecorded answer in Galatians 6:7–8, "Do not be deceived, God is not mocked; for whatever a man sows, this he will also reap. For the one who sows to his own flesh shall from the flesh reap corruption" (NASB).

God's answer resounded in our minds with unmistakable clarity, "Don't blame Me. I already told you not to do what you did. I prerecorded My warning of what would happen if you did. But you did it anyway!"

"That's no excuse," God thunders at our whimpering excuse

making. How often we pray, "Oh, God, I didn't know!" and God answers in disgust, "That's no excuse!"

Then He adds, "Especially you theologians, you pastors, you Bible study leaders, you Sunday school teachers, you who read my Bible devotionally, don't feign ignorance! You have the whole Bible in your own language, and I have prerecorded all that information for you." And God reminds us of His recorded warning, "For unto whomsoever much is given, of him shall be much required" (Luke 12:48).

"I didn't change My command just because you live in the twentieth century," God declares, "with its humanism and 'whatever-feels-good-do-it' philosophy creeping into and, yes, almost overgrowing, today's Christian church."

Today, one of God's commands that is most distorted is, "Let none deal treacherously against the wife of his youth" (Mal. 2:15).

An acquaintance of ours has had affair after affair because his wife "is getting old and fat." Continuously brainwashed by this concept in every conceivable media, he has asked himself, "What is wrong with being satisfied with younger, firmer flesh?" And, worst of all, his wife is taking all the blame on herself because he has convinced her that she is the guilty one for being this way. But God has not rescinded His command, "Be ye holy; for I am holy" (1 Pet. 1:16) just because we live in the twentieth century!

Today, we have the opposite problem of wives out in the marketplace and, as they grow older, associating with men with fresh minds and younger bodies. And this situation can be pleasant to them also. It is therefore just as important for a wife to obey God and not "deal treacherously against the [husband] of [her] youth."

One of the most common complaints I hear from aging wives confirms what a medical doctor told me years ago. "As the husband grows older," he said, "he tends to settle down, pull back from the action, while the wife still feels full of vigor, vision, and plans for the future." But this seemingly common problem does not give her the right to gravitate toward, and be fulfilled by, younger men either.

"Enjoy life with the woman whom you love all the days of your fleeting life," says the author of Ecclesiastes (9:9, NASB). Enjoy! Don't stoically "put up with" each other because God commanded it, but in love and fellowship enjoy each other!

"But I promised My peace," God's voice so often consoles me. Frequently, it is not His scolding voice, but it is God's reassuring voice calming and soothing my anxious spirit.

I had just one week to get ready for my first trip to Japan and was frantically trying to get everything done. When I prayed about and shopped for the raincoat and the dress I would need for speaking, God explicitly directed my thinking to a familiar passage in Matthew 6:25. Turning to it, I read again Jesus' words, "For this reason I say to you, do not be anxious for your life, *as to* what you shall eat, or what you shall drink; nor for your body, *as to* what you shall put on. Is not life more than food, and the body than clothing?" (NASB).

I had His answer! Breathing a heartfelt prayer of "Thank You, Lord!" I relaxed in His prerecorded answer to my anxiety and decided to make my old raincoat do. (It never rained once while I was there.) Then I trusted Him to lead me to just the dress I needed—which He did—almost miraculously.

Recorded in my Bible's margin by Matthew 6:25 are these words, "I awoke early the day before going to Japan with a smile on my face and complete peace in my whole being. Anxious for nothing!"

The next year God reinforced this prerecorded answer to me at the Mukti Ramabai Mission in India. My husband and I had parted the day before at the Bombay Airport, where he boarded a plane to return to America because of illness. As I sat alone outside the mission gate watching the dawn break, apprehension filled my heart as I was praying about being left without him to do all the speaking that week at the National Prayer Assembly of India. The air was filled with the noise of a thousand birds as a pale sliver of moon gave way to the pink dawn.

Again God directed my mind back to that Scripture about anxiety in Matthew 6, and I turned to read it. His answer, "Look at the birds of the air," sharpened my awareness and intensified the cacophony of bird sounds while I continued listening to Jesus. "They do not sow, neither do they reap, nor gather into barns, and *yet* your heavenly Father feeds them. Are *you* not worth much more than they?" (v. 26, NASB). Oh, yes, He would take care of me! His answers about anxiety had been there all the time. I had even claimed them myriads of times before. But when I needed them again—and asked— God guided me to His prerecorded answer, fresh for that day.

"Just trust Me," came God's reassuring voice after we had prayed many months for our daughter Jan to be able to conceive after ten years of a childless marriage. He guided me to read once again the faith chapter, Hebrews 11. I was surprised as the list of males of faith suddenly changed to a female of faith, "Sarah herself received ability to conceive [literally, the power for the laying down of seed], even beyond the proper time of life, since *she* considered Him faithful who had promised; therefore, also, there was born" (vv. 11, 12a, NASB).

Therefore, to Sarah, because of her faith and her husband, Abraham, "full of faith," was born a child. God had kept His promise. And to our Jan, because of her faith and the faith of her husband, Skip, was born our Jennifer.

"Oh, I have just the advice you need," God said as He gently led me to 2 Corinthians 2:14 the morning of the seminar in London during my second British Isles tour. The night before, the committee had been concerned and prayed much that the peace marchers, who had a reputation for disrupting vocally and lying down in the aisles, had secured tickets for the seminar. Slightly unnerved, all I could pray that morning was, "Oh, God, make me what You want me to *be.*"

And His prerecorded answer as I reached for my Bible was, "But thanks be to God, who always leads us in His triumph in Christ, and *manifests through us the sweet aroma of the knowledge of Him in every place"* (2 Cor. 2:14, NASB).

"Oh, God, please make me just a sweet aroma of Jesus," I cried. And He answered my prayer. There was not one disruption all day, even though all the seats were taken, indicating to us that the peace marchers were there. The sweet aroma of Jesus! Prerecorded for me!

I prayed this same verse before every secular interview of the tour. It was the first arm of "Mission: England," and whole days were filled with interviews by the secular press, radio, and TV. I knew I wasn't smart enough to answer their questions about President Reagan's Central American policy or the nuclear arms race; so before each interview, I prayed a simple prayer, "Oh, God, let them see only Jesus in me. Only Jesus!" And He answered. The deep spiritual questions they continuously asked astounded me. Never once did they expect me to solve America's foreign policy.

Not knowing why, our daughter Jan had given me this same

verse—because God had given it to her to give me—as I left
for that speaking tour. The sweet aroma of Jesus—prerecorded
for us both to find!

I struggle to close this section because of the hundreds of
illustrations I have to leave out; but here are a few more of
the different tones of voice God uses when answering my
prayers with His prerecorded answers.

"I knew you were going to hurt," God tenderly answers our
anguished cry for help, "so I wrote these tender words of
comfort to heal your broken heart." Then He sends us to
some of His prerecorded words, which almost seem to enfold
us in His loving arms.

"Let Me explain that," God calmly instructs my befuddled
mind with His voice of omniscience. Then He directs me to
His prerecorded answer that clears up the puzzle and enlight-
ens my confused mind.

"Speak with My authority," God firmly commanded in June
of 1981. It was my first seminar in London; and the night
before, a "scary awe" came over me as I looked over Westminster Hall, where the seminar was to be held for those twenty-
five hundred women. A tremendous reluctance swept over
me at the thought of my having the audacity to tell these
lovely ladies they needed to change.

The next morning, I asked God for His Word for me. While
I was reading in Titus 2, He firmly assured me with His prerecorded answer: "These things speak and exhort and reprove
with all authority. Let no one disregard you" (v. 15, NASB).

From the time I started teaching, there was no sense of
anything but God doing His great work in our midst; and I
had indescribable freedom to speak and exhort and reprove
all that day because God had assured me of His authority
with His prerecorded answer!

"I've just been waiting to share that secret with you," God
eagerly answers my searching mind. And then my heart burns
within me, as with the two on the Emmaus Road that first
Easter (Luke 24:32), while He opens His treasure of wisdom
and knowledge and pulls back the curtain on deep and exciting
mysteries from His Word. Mysteries that have been there
since the foundation of the world but are just now mine—
because I asked.

"I thought you'd never ask." Of all the ways God answers,
this probably is the one He most often repeats. God almost
sighs in relief as we finally get around to including Him in

our search for advice and instruction. "But why did you wait so long," He sighs wearily, "when I had the prerecorded answers ready for you all along?"

Yes, God's voices in answering me are as varied as my needs, frequently surprising me, but always giving me just what I need or deserve. God is not remote, speaking from somewhere up in the sky, but is always present with me while I turn to His word for His answers.

Hindrances to Accepting God's Prerecorded Answers

Unfortunately, there are hindrances to receiving God's prerecorded answers which we have built up within ourselves.

Disbelief in the authenticity of the Bible frequently keeps people from believing God's prerecorded answers. Disbelief in the authority of God's Word also can be a stumbling block to accepting His prerecorded answers.

Theological hang-ups also can hinder our acceptance of God's answers to our prayers. Most of us are hemmed in by a theological system either from the denomination into which we were born, the church we chose as an adult, or from gullibly accepting what others have taught us. We have put God in our little theological boxes; and when His answer in the Bible doesn't quite fit our well-worked-out doctrinal system, we have difficulty accepting it.

Rebellion. Even though we agree theologically with God's answer and know we should accept it, many times we rebel against His will for us and are too stubborn to accept His prerecorded answer.

Not applying it personally is also a hindrance to the effectiveness in our lives of God's prerecorded answers. It is far easier to apply that reproof, correction, or instruction to the ones we are teaching, our congregation, or even our mates, children, or acquaintances. But it is only as we are willing to accept His answer for us personally that it can accomplish that which God intended it to do when He recorded it. "Blessed are those who hear the word of God and observe it" (Luke 11:28, NASB).

Interact with the Author

Since God is personally present when we receive His prerecorded answer from the Bible, it is logical that He expects us to interact with Him about what He has said. And since this is the only book in which the author is always present while it is being read, it also is true that this is the only book where a personal interaction with the Author, God, is necessary.

The Bible differs from all other books ever written in that it is alive. Hebrews 4:12 says, "The word of God is quick and powerful and sharper than any two-edged sword, . . . and is a discerner of the thoughts and intents of the heart." This is only possible because God Himself, its Author, is active in its convicting, enlightening, and instructing process. Thus, the Bible can be applied practically only through spiritual involvement with God Himself. And this interaction is prayer.

This is not true of any other book. When we obey the traffic rule book and stop our car when the light turns red, there is no personal involvement with the person who at some time decided we "stop on red" and "go on green." Also, with textbooks, it is not necessary to become personally involved with the author in order to put into practice the laws, information, rules, or suggestions he or she is teaching. Learning and using a mathematical formula is not dependent upon a personal relationship with its originator. Not so with the Bible. There must be the reader's spiritual response to the Author to ensure adequate and meaningful application of its precepts.

Three steps are necessary in using God's prerecorded answer effectively: (1) accept it, (2) respond to its Author, and (3) live it. We frequently want to bypass number 2 and resolutely set our jaws and grit our teeth declaring, "I will not," or stoically set out to obey its commands. But it is only when we involve the Author of these rules and instructions that we receive the wisdom, grace, strength, power, and, most important, the desire to apply them.

But one difficulty today is that we are basically teaching our children, Sunday school pupils, Bible study groups, and church members only numbers 1 and 3. We are trying to impose the application of the Bible's laws and rules on others and ourselves without a relationship with and a response to the Author, God.

Then we wonder why God's Word is a seemingly dead set of dos and do nots, why its precepts are compared with the teachings of other books, why we rationalize away its truths in the light of what other books say, and why we test its veracity in the light of other writings.

We must respond personally to God about what He has said to us—asking forgiveness for that specific sin, staying quietly in His presence while He cleanses us, seeing ourselves in contrast to His holiness, imploring Him to make us more like the Jesus He just showed us. Or remaining in silence until we feel the love for which we asked come from Him. Or waiting for His filling with power to accomplish what His answer just directed us to do.

There is no other author who discerns and judges the thoughts and the intents of our hearts and scrutinizes the spiritual, emotional, and intellectual aspects of our lives. Nor do we stand before any other author stripped and bare and fully exposed, with nothing concealed (Heb. 4:13). Thus, no other book consistently and without fail can have prerecorded answers for the immediate and specific needs of the reader, for no other author is actively involved in the inmost and hidden self of the reader.

To be confronted by God's prerecorded answers in the Bible is to be confronted by God Himself.

Closing Prayer

Father, thank You for prerecording most of the answers I shall ever need. Forgive me for neglecting to read the Bible for Your prerecorded answers to my prayers. Teach me to submerge myself in Your prerecorded instructions and commands for me and then to interact with You about them. Lord, I now promise You I will seek, accept, and obey Your prerecorded answers for me.

In Jesus' name, **Amen.**

5

You Have Not Fulfilled My Requirements

Have you ever wondered why God answers no to some of your prayers? He may be saying, "You have not fulfilled My requirements. You do not qualify for My answer!" This is the greatest secret of unanswered prayer.

Many Christians sincerely desire to have power in prayer, prayer that produces changed people and circumstances here on earth, but they are bewildered when nothing happens. They pray earnest, fervent prayers; but God does not seem to answer. However, when His answer is no, He may be saying, "There are some missing qualifiers in your life."

God decreed these "if," "when," and "because" conditions in our lives before the foundation of the world, and His no answer may actually be, "When you do, then I will."

Because You Do, Then I Will

First John 3:22 gives us one of God the Father's basic rules for answering or not answering our prayers. It is the Father's "then":

And whatsoever we ask, we receive of him, *because* we keep his commandments, and do those things that are pleasing in his sight.

The Father's approval or disapproval of our actions determines whether or not He will grant our prayer requests. Since both words *keep* and *do* in this verse of Scripture are in the continuous present tense in the Greek, power in prayer is conditioned not by an occasional burst of obedience but by lives that consistently please Him. *Then* He promises that we will receive that for which we ask.

One of the numerous "thens" in Scripture that determine answered prayer is in 2 Chronicles 7:14. God told Solomon that if His people would "humble themselves, pray, seek [his] face, and turn from their wicked ways; *then* [he would] hear from heaven, and will forgive their sin, and will heal their land." When they did, He would.

David, after his deep sin with Bathsheba, knew and prayed God's *then* principle for the return of fruitfulness in his life. He was aware of the order God required. It was when he acknowledged his sin, deeply repented, begged God to create in him a clean heart, and asked God to restore the joy of His salvation, that only *then* could he again teach transgressors of God's ways and sinners would be converted (Ps. 51).

We seem to be so unaware of God's "thens" when we pray. But the Bible clearly tells us that God can answer our prayers only when we have been willing to be and to do what He requires. "When you keep My commandments and do the things which are pleasing in My sight," says the Lord, "only then will you receive that for which you have asked" (see 1 John 3:22).

If You Do, Then I Will

Recently, I have been basing our "What Happens When We Pray" seminars on Jesus' words in John 15:7, in which He gives His two all-inclusive *if* conditions for answered prayer, "If ye abide in me, and [if] my words abide in you, ye shall ask what ye will, and it shall be done unto you."

These words, "shall be done unto you," contain the most powerful prayer promise in the New Testament, according to G. Campbell Morgan. They actually involve God's creative power, and they are equivalent in power to the account of God's creation of the universe in the Book of Genesis.

In March 1971, as I was studying this verse, I became overwhelmed at the thought of the power Jesus was promising His followers—and us. "Lord, how much power did it take to create the universe?" I prayed. Then my mind boggled as I tried to envision the tiny percentage of the universe we have explored or even measured. And His power had to be greater than the combined power of all He created. I tried in vain to comprehend the power it took to create it by the word of His mouth. I wept as I prayed, "Father, I want that power in prayer." Slowly, I implored, "Teach me—and break me—until I have it!"

This promised power is not a deep, dark, unobtainable mystery available only to a privileged few. It is there for all Christians today. However, Jesus did say that there are conditions for obtaining it. There are things that must be evident in our lives in order for God to answer our prayers.

What are these qualifiers? In John 15:7, Jesus clearly identifies them for us. Jesus' first condition for this prayer power is: "*If* ye abide in me." Just before He was crucified, He spoke these words to His disciples in His discourse on the vine and the branches. So abiding in Jesus is first being intrinsically, organically connected to Him, the vine. Of course, only true Christians qualify as those who are abiding in Him. And nowhere in the New Testament is there a promise of intercessory prayer power to any but those who are true Christians—who can pray "in the name of Jesus."

In addition, to abide in Jesus is to receive sustenance, strength, and power from Him as branches from a vine. It is resting securely in Him not only when all is going well but also in those dark times when we are being pruned and broken—this is abiding in Jesus.

The second *if* qualifier from Jesus in John 15:7 is "[If] my words abide in you." If we want this prayer power, all His words must abide in us, take up residence in us. And we must obey them and live by them.

What are Jesus' words? First, when Jesus was praying to His Father at the close of His life here on earth, He told God that He had given to us all the words the Father had given Him (John 17:8). Second, "But the Comforter, which is the

Holy [Spirit], whom the Father will send in my name, he shall teach you all things, and bring all things to your remembrance, whatsoever I have said unto you" (John 14:26). These things recalled and taught by the Holy Spirit were written down as the rest of the New Testament. Third, between His resurrection and ascension, Jesus opened the Old Testament to His followers in the light of His life, death, and resurrection. In other words, the Holy Scripture is the word of Jesus.

All of this is summed up in 1 John 3:24, "And the one who *keeps* His commandments abides in Him" (NASB). It is obedience to all His commandments that proves we are abiding in Him—Jesus' first requirement for prayer power.

A few years ago, I had a too-close-for-comfort brush with someone who, although knowing full well what Jesus' words on infidelity are, certainly was not letting them abide in him, nor was he obeying them.

I learned of this when our son, Kurt, then a college freshman, phoned and with an unusual urgency in his voice asked, "Mom, can you bring the car to me?"

When I pulled up at the college, he got in, slammed the door, and blurted, "Do the prayer chains pray at night, Mom?"

Fearing the worst, I assured him, "They do if you need them. Why? What's wrong?"

"Well, this freshman girl in my class is having an affair with a local pastor. I told her it is wrong, and she has to break it off. Well, she's afraid to go alone. So I'm going to take her to see him and help her."

My heart sank. "Honey," I promised, "the prayer chains *will* pray for you tonight!" Which they did—and his daddy and I—all the time they were gone.

Finally, they came back to our house, and we sat around the kitchen table listening to Kurt's recounting of the evening. Suddenly he said, "I told the pastor, 'She's only a college freshman and may not have known better, but you—you have a theological education. Boy,' " Kurt swung his fist in the air to make his point, " 'I wouldn't want to be in *your* shoes when you meet God!' "

All of the teaching in the Bible on infidelity was being absolutely disregarded by this teacher of the Word. I wonder how many of the pastor's prayers were being answered by God.

In our prayer seminars, we call Jesus' second "if" condition—His words abiding in us—"prerequisites to power in prayer." We include His words about being forgiven, forgiving one another, praying in God's will, making sure it is God to whom we have drawn nigh, personal prayer life of the pray-er, and actual praying of intercessory prayers. I teach all my personal prayer chain, twenty-four-hour clock, and metro prayer chain people these prerequisites either in a seminar or require them to study and apply them from the book, *What Happens When Women Pray.* For without obeying Jesus' words, there is no power in their prayers—and their praying is futile.

Of course, Jesus' words include His declaration in John 3:3 of the necessity of being born again. Without this first step, there is no obedience to Jesus' words, thus no abiding, and thus no power in prayer. Jesus also said, "No man cometh unto the Father, but by me" (John 14:6). Without this required step, none of the promises in the Bible pertaining to answered prayer apply.

Lord, Is It I?

I was in for a surprise last September at my board's fall kickoff "Lord, Change Me" retreat. As we all sat around sharing our experiences of the latter part of the summer with its struggles, words like *desert, dearth,* and *dry* kept coming up. They expressed exactly the way I had felt in August, even to the point of toying with the idea of giving up my ministry. But I had been unaware of what had caused this unusual response in me.

We began our retreat by taking our Bibles, going apart by ourselves, and each reading the same portion of Scripture silently until God stopped us on a particular thought. As we came together to share what God had said to us individually, all but one board member had been reproved by God's Word (1 Tim. 3:16). Mentioned were sins of commission, omission, attitudes toward a splitting church, **and** a critical spirit that had crept into my board members' lives, which they, weeping, confessed. And I joined my board members confessing the sin that God had shown me of thinking I had the right to shut Jesus' door on my life as I chose—which I had been thinking about doing that last difficult month.

Just before leaving the retreat early to go to Chattanooga

for a seminar, I told them I now understood why the summer had been so difficult for them and me. It was sin in their lives and mine. Not those big "dirty dozen" sins—just those everyday attitudes and actions that had closed heaven's door, and thus its power, to us. In the words of Peter to the Christians of his day, we were reminded that "the eyes of the Lord *are* over the righteous, and his ears *are open* unto their prayers: but the face of the Lord *is* against them that do evil" (1 Pet. 3:12).

Now, these board members are the main prayer supporters of my ministry. And even if they had prayed for me, God would not have answered—because they weren't fulfilling His condition in Psalm 66:18 that He will not even hear us if we regard iniquity in our hearts.

Once again, we had learned the truth of David's Psalm 24:3–4, "Who may ascend into the hill of the LORD? And who may stand in His holy place? He who has clean hands and a pure heart" (NASB). But because we confessed our failures openly and honestly as sin before God, I went to Chattanooga to minister with great joy, freedom, *and God's power*—while they prayed. Yes, God has His requirements in our lives for prayer power.

At my board's next executive committee meeting, we were struggling with a financial need for our newsletter. We opened with a period of prayer for about an hour; and, as each one prayed, the theme seemed to be: Is it *my* attitude, *my* sin, *my* prayerlessness, *my* lack of faith that is keeping You from answering our prayers about our financial need? Lord, is it *I?*

Isaiah clearly explained God's response to the prayers of His people who were living in sin and rebellion: "So when you spread out your hands in prayer, I will hide My eyes from you, Yes, even though you multiply prayers, I will not listen. Your hands are full of bloodshed" (Isa. 1:15, NASB).

Are you lacking God's power in your life? Could it be unidentified and unconfessed sin?

The Holy Spirit Thwarted

All three persons of the Trinity work in accordance with certain principles when answering our prayers. Most of these principles are the qualifiers in our lives, which God expects us to meet.

The person of the Trinity about whom Paul is writing in Ephesians 3:20 is, of course, God the Holy Spirit. He is working in response to, according to, our praying; but He is only able to work to the extent that we do not hinder Him by the sins in our lives.

According to the Bible, there are ways we can offend the Holy Spirit that will keep our prayers from being answered because, of course, these are all sin.

We can *grieve* the Holy Spirit. As Paul in Ephesians 4:25–32 lists the sins that must be banished from the Christian's life, he says abruptly in the middle of the list, "And do not grieve the Holy Spirit" (v. 30, NASB). Do not cause him pain, distress, or grief by denying in practice His indwelling, holy presence. This is what we do when we commit this and other sins.

A pastor called one Saturday night and said, "We're studying your book *Lord, Change Me!* and are having a great time learning so much. But," he paused, "I have a question for you. Are you Superwoman? Do you ever have any struggles? Are you perfect?"

Shocked, I explained, "Oh, no! I confess my sins daily! Many times a day! I do strive to be holy, but the more I do the more God shows me my sin."

Every morning before teaching or speaking, I spend as much time as necessary waiting on God in silence after praying, "Search me, O God, . . . and see if there be any wicked way in me" (Ps. 139:23–24). This searching is not morbid introspection, but one of the jobs of the Holy Spirit. It gives God a chance to bring to our attention those little attitudes, thoughts, or motives that slip by so easily without our recognizing them.

If I am living with any known sin—pride, wrong attitudes or priorities, or disobedience to where He is sending me—I am going to be ministering in my own strength, and there will be no moving of God's Spirit in power in my seminar. Oh, I can mouth the right words and give the correct illustrations, but the power to move lives isn't there.

In another country, a young evangelist, whose wife is physically handicapped, came to me for prayer. While traveling away from home, he was having a difficult time working with the active young women on his committees. He shared the constant temptation he was experiencing. My answer to him was simply, "You have a tremendously bright future, but there is no way God will play games with you. He will not tolerate sin in your life. And if it is there, He absolutely will not hear and answer your prayers."

Speaking at a Successful Living convention in Canada in 1978, I suddenly felt a lack of God's power. Then I became aware of an attitude in me that was sin. I recorded in my diary, "It is good for me to be aware that I cannot entertain any un-Christlike attitudes and still have the power essential for God's moving in my ministry." The greatest deterrent to my sinning or allowing unconfessed sin in my life is knowing that there will be no power in my ministry. This is my responsibility.

Whenever there has been any lack of His power in a seminar or on my board, my first question always is, "Lord, is it I? Do You mean that the exceeding abundant things I asked You to do, You cannot do because of me?" And He again reminds me that He is able to do only according to the capacity I permit Him by my cleansed lifestyle.

In addition to grieving the Holy Spirit, we also can *quench* Him. In 1 Thessalonians 5:12–22, Paul lists instructions for living for Christians in that day and for us today. In the middle of this list of admonitions, he abruptly states, "Do not quench the Spirit" (v. 19, NASB).

What does it mean to quench? It is to put out a fire. How often I have agonized in prayer before a convention for the Holy Spirit to descend in power, then felt Him beginning to come—only to have someone piously "move the order of the day." And the quenching successfully has taken place. I would go home heartbroken because I so desperately wanted God to set us on fire—with His fire. He tried so many times to answer this prayer, but people just would not let Him.

Or, who of us has not been in a church service when God really started to move, only to have the order of the service proceed as usual—or dismiss on time? The Holy Spirit quenched. And that is sin, which must break God's heart.

Peter tells us, surprisingly, in 1 Peter 3:7, that a husband's prayers can be *hindered* if he does not have the right attitude toward his wife. To hinder means to impede a person by putting an obstacle in his path or breaking up the road in front of him as he travels, detaining him unnecessarily. So a wrong attitude, which in God's eyes is sin, can impede our answers to prayer.

The night before a prayer seminar in Texas, I spent a half-hour asking God to bring to my mind every attitude, thought, and action that would hinder His working in the seminar. Then, any attitudes, thoughts, or action against anybody whom I needed to forgive. I then asked for forgiveness from God and forgave those who had sinned against me. I experienced a tremendous sense of being completely clean on the inside!

The next day as I was teaching about keeping our pipe line to God clean so as not to hinder our prayers, I actually felt as if the inside of my "pipe line" was like highly polished mirrorlike metal. Nothing was hindering His power—which was very evident as at least half of the participants prayed aloud making sure that they had a personal relationship with Jesus (including a prominent local pastor). The difference is whether I provide a clear channel—or one with hindering friction.

Yes, the Holy Spirit is a person, the third member of the Trinity, who can be quenched, grieved, hindered, vexed, resisted, ignored, blasphemed against, lied to, and offended. Even His work of trying to rescue the sinner can be despised and rejected. And all of these are sins which will stop God's power from working in us through answers to our prayers. This, of course, is just the opposite of being filled with, and walking in, the Spirit.

God's Spirit is sorrowful and sore-troubled at the ignoring, resisting, and despising of His work on the part of those He is trying to rescue from sin and lead into a joyous Christian life. But, amazingly, no matter how hurt He is at our sinning against Him, instead of retaliating or withdrawing, the Holy Spirit constantly reproves and woos us back. How opposite to the way we humans respond to each other when we are offended!

Holiness

If we expect God to answer our prayers, we must meet His requirement of holiness. The triune God expects this of us. God the Father commands, "Be ye holy; for I am holy"

(1 Pet. 1:16). Paul writes in Romans 8:29 that we are predestined "to be conformed to the image of his Son"—Jesus, who, although tempted in all things as we are, yet was without sin—to be holy (Heb. 4:15). Then, "Be filled with the [Holy] Spirit" (Eph. 5:18). Holiness is the fundamental attribute of God and His requirement for us.

At a seminar in Perth, Australia, as I sent us all to read Galatians 5 and 6 until God spoke to each of us, I prayed, "Oh, God, give me something very personal—just for me today." And He directed my eyes across the page to Ephesians, chapter 1. There it was—His word for me. "Just as He chose us in Him before the foundation of the world, *that* we should be holy and blameless before Him" (1:4, NASB). His requirement for me!

Yes, holiness. Anything less in my life is sin. And "if I regard iniquity in my heart, the Lord will not hear me" (Ps. 66:18). So, here is the reason for many of God's seemingly no answers.

"Is it all hopeless?" you ask. Oh, no! Identifying and confessing our sins does produce the holy life that is necessary for God to hear and answer our prayers.

Lists of Sins

Perhaps you have difficulty identifying the things in your life that really are sin. Well, the Bible has the answer for you. The most powerful tool I use in my prayer seminars is a list of twenty-three portions of Scripture which, as with all Scripture, if not obeyed, is sin. I explain that according to James 4:17, "To him [or her] that knoweth to do good, and doeth it not, to him [or her] it is sin."

In my thirteen years of full-time seminar ministry, I have seen a consistent pattern in at least 99 percent of the participants praying aloud in their groups of four, asking God to forgive specific sins. This, by the way, is the first prayer I ask to be prayed aloud; and we estimate that approximately half of those who attend our seminars have never prayed in public before. The secret is the Bible's power to reprove sin (2 Tim. 3:15).

The Bible abounds in the things we should do, but don't; and those things we should not do, but do—thus, we are found guilty of the sins of omission and commission.

Colossians 3:5-9 covers these two categories of sin. The first is the list of things we should not do. And if we do any of them, we sin before God. Take time right now to read them slowly, pausing to consider each sin as it may apply to you personally:

> Therefore consider the members of your earthly body as dead to immorality, impurity, passion, evil desire, and greed, which amounts to idolatry. For it is on account of these things that the wrath of God will come, and in them you also once walked, when you were living in them. But *now* you also, put them all aside: anger, wrath, malice, slander, and abusive speech from your mouth. Do not lie to one another, since you laid aside the old self with its evil practices (NASB).

Then Paul goes on at verse 12 to list those things that we should do; and, if we fail to do them, we sin:

> And so, as those who have been chosen of God, holy and beloved, put on . . . compassion, kindness, humility, gentleness and patience; bearing with one another, and forgiving each other, whoever has a complaint against any one; just as the Lord forgave you, so also should you. And beyond all these things put on love, which is the perfect bond of unity. And let the peace of Christ rule in your hearts, to which indeed you were called in one body; and be thankful. Let the word of Christ richly dwell within you, with all wisdom teaching and admonishing one another with psalms and hymns and spiritual songs, singing with thankfulness in your hearts to God. And whatever you do in word or deed, do all in the name of the Lord Jesus, giving thanks through Him to God the Father (Col. 3:12-17, NASB).

Now that we have considered these scriptural requirements, we are responsible for living up to them. It is awesome to realize that failing to do any of the above constitutes sin in God's eyes.

Jesus, in Mark 7:21-22, gave to us His very revealing list of things that come forth from us and defile us. He included: "evil thoughts and fornications, thefts, murders, adulteries, deeds of coveting and wickedness, as well as deceit, sensuality, envy, slander, pride and foolishness" (NASB). What a combination of the "big," blatant sins and the "everyday" sins of the Christian!

Then Paul gave us an unnervingly specific list of sins in Galatians 5:19–21:

Now the deeds of the flesh are evident, which are: immorality, impurity, sensuality, idolatry, sorcery, enmities, strife, jealousy, outbursts of anger, disputes, dissensions, factions, envyings, drunkenness, carousings, and things like these, of which I forewarn you just as I have forewarned you that those who practice such things shall not inherit the kingdom of God (NASB).

Yes, James 4:17 clearly tells us that now that we know to do good, when we don't do it—to us, it is sin. Not shortcomings. Not personality quirks. Sin!

Did you find your "pet" sin in those verses of Scripture? Was your "secret" sin, or sins, exposed by one of them? *If so, you have one of the reasons for God not answering your prayers—you do not qualify!*

But the great fact is that we don't have to stay in the condition where God answers our prayers with no because there is sin in our lives. The Bible emphatically states that "if we confess our sins, he is faithful and just to forgive us our sins, and to cleanse us from all unrighteousness" (1 John 1:9).

While I was on vacation in 1983, God showed me this tremendous verse, "Therefore, having these promises, beloved, let us cleanse ourselves from all defilement of flesh and spirit, perfecting holiness in the fear of God" (2 Cor. 7:1, NASB).

The required order is God's: identify, admit, confess, ask God to forgive—and forgiveness!

Of course, God has His requirements for our power in prayer. But He also has the answer—forgiveness—when we ask!

Closing Prayer

Father, You seem to be answering no to my prayer requests— or not answering at all. Could it be unidentified and unconfessed sin, or sins, in my life that is keeping You from answering my prayers? Lord, please show me which ones. Oh, God, I do confess all my sins! Please forgive me! Cleanse me!

In Jesus' name, **Amen.**

6

WHEN GOD ANSWERS . . .

Repent

When we have prayed, "Father, I have sinned," how does God answer us? Does He say, "Now that you have confessed the fact that you have sinned, it will be all right"? Oh, no. God then commands us to "Repent!"

A bewildered wife called me asking for prayer. She said that her husband was sleeping with another woman, then getting up the next morning and asking God to forgive him. He told his wife it was OK because God always forgives us when we ask Him to. "Is this true?" the wife questioned. "Does he have a right as a Christian to live this way?"

"No," I replied, and then shared a part of Romans 6 with her: "Are we to continue in sin that grace might increase? May it never be!" (vv. 1–2). "Therefore do not let sin reign in your mortal body that you should obey its lusts, and do not go on presenting the members of your body to sin as instruments of unrighteousness; but present yourselves to God as those alive from the dead, and your members as instruments of righteousness to God" (vv. 12–13, NASB).

After we have identified a specific sin in our lives as sin and have admitted it to God in prayer, we humans are prone to say to ourselves, "Now, just forget it," or "Oh, that's really not a sin." Or we may say, "You really didn't mean to hurt anybody," or "That's not such a bad sin." But God says, "Repent!"

When we have admitted a sin, God never says, "Oh, that's all right, My child. Let's just forget it now, and you get on with your life." Oh, no. He doesn't say, "That's that," and close the curtain on the whole thing. He expects continued action on both our part and His. Our part in the next act is to repent.

Jesus and Repentance

Why repent? Because Jesus said so—to both Christians and non-Christians.

Jesus had been back in heaven after His ascension for approximately sixty years when He sent messages to His churches on earth to repent. The apostle John, recording these messages in Revelation 2 and 3, startles us with the force and frequency of Jesus' command, "Repent!"

When the Son of God began His ministry on earth, He proclaimed the same message, "Repent!" He came into Galilee preaching, "The time is fulfilled, and the kingdom of God is at hand: repent ye, and believe the gospel" (Mark 1:15).

Even His forerunner, John the Baptist, prepared the way for Jesus by calling the religious leaders of the day to repentance. He cried, "Repent ye: for the kingdom of heaven is at hand" (Matt. 3:2).

Jesus, also, seeing sinful men in contrast to His Father's holiness and His own sinlessness, commanded them to repent throughout His earthly ministry. He was so disturbed by the sin He saw on earth that, in His Sermon on the Mount, He actually said it was better to cut off the offending member of our body than for the whole body to perish in hell (Matt. 5:29).

Then, after dying and paying the price for all sin, some of the final words the resurrected Jesus gave to His followers are recorded in Luke 24:46–47, where He admonishes them to keep on preaching repentance to all nations,

And He said to them, "Thus it is written, that the Christ should suffer and rise again from the dead the third day; and that repentance for forgiveness of sins should be proclaimed in His name to all the nations, beginning at Jerusalem" (NASB).

Then Peter, so fresh from his own repentance, immediately obeyed Jesus' command in his very first sermon, admonishing the nonbelieving men of Israel, "Repent, and let each of you be baptized in the name of Jesus Christ for the forgiveness of your sins" (Acts 2:38, NASB; see also Acts 3:18, 19).

So the purpose of Jesus' coming, His preaching, and His death and resurrection was that repentance for forgiveness of sins could be proclaimed in His name to everyone, everywhere. And it is still His concern as He lives back in heaven with His Father.

Right now, Jesus is at the right hand of the Father interceding for us. For what is He praying? Only for our strength, power, grace, and guidance? I think not. For, since He had to send instructions to the young churches to repent, what might He be praying for us today? Is He interceding for me, for you, for our churches—right now—that we will repent?

"What Do You Mean, Repent?"

What is repentance? It is much more than a quick "forgive me" prayer. It involves three things: being truly sorrowful for the sin, actively turning away from that sin, and bringing forth fruit in keeping with repentance.

Being really sorry for the sin is to be absolutely devastated by the thought of it. It was when the men of Israel heard Peter raise his voice and recount their sins that they were "pierced to the heart" and cried out, asking the apostle what to do. Peter's reply was, "Repent!"

True repentance is not being afraid of the consequences of sin, but horrified at the sin itself. In my childhood home, repentance was my own father literally hitting his head against the wall because of what he had done to my mother. After years of being untrue to her when he traveled as a state highway contractor, he finally confessed his sin to her. Why did he confess? Because he saw his sin in contrast to my dear mother's holy life before God. When he came home from his week on the road, he told her he could almost see an angel hovering over her. It was her godlike holiness in contrast to his lustful wickedness that led him to confess—and change his lifestyle.

A Christian leader, who had an affair with his secretary for several years, shared that it had been his wife's constant quest for holiness, too, that had made his life so unbearable he finally confessed his sin to her. But rather than confess, at first, he frequently had contemplated suicide and did attempt it, but failed when stopped by the police. Writhing in agony on his bed, he confessed the filthy, lurid details of his sin.

Yes, after acknowledging our sin as sin comes the step of repentance—being horrified and devastated by the sinning and begging God for a clean heart once again.

I have watched this pattern of repentance in thirteen years of "What Happens When We Pray" seminars. The first prerequisite for prayer power in our lives that we study is "no known unconfessed sin in the life of the pray-er." Before we begin our first audible prayer time in small groups, I read a list of commonly practiced sins from the Bible—such as pride, lying, lust, wasting time, bitterness, money as our god, corrupt communication, and being a fake. As the Holy Spirit convicts us through God's Word, there almost always is deep repentance, with all confessing and many weeping. Frequently, this prayer of repentance goes on far into our scheduled morning break time.

Although seeing our sin may make us uncomfortable or even embarrassed, Paul tells us that this process is good for us. After sending a letter to the Christians in Corinth condemning their sins, Paul wrote a second time, rejoicing in the fact that it was godly sorrow that had produced repentance in them: "For I see that that letter caused you sorrow, though only for a while—I now rejoice, not that you [Christians] were made sorrowful, but that you were made sorrowful to the point of repentance; for you were made sorrowful according to the will of God, . . . For the sorrow that is according to the will of God produces a repentance without regret" (2 Cor. 7:8–10, NASB).

Turning away from the sin is the second step in true repentance. There is no real repentance without this step. For years, I have asked God daily to search my heart and show me my sins. And I find it relatively easy to admit that these un-Christlike attitudes and actions are sin and to ask for forgiveness.

And I truly do regret having said, done, or thought certain things, but I do not actually repent until I turn away from them. Proverbs 28:13 says, "He who conceals his transgressions will not prosper, But he who confesses *and forsakes* them will find compassion" (NASB).

The husband who thought he could sleep with another woman every night and then be forgiven the next day did not understand God's requirements. The only words God had for him were "Repent—and prove your repentance by a change of actions!"

Third, *true repentance is bringing "forth fruit in keeping with . . . repentance"* (Matt. 3:8, NASB). It is not only turning *from* something, but also it is turning *to* something.

Before getting up early one summer morning at our cottage, I was praying, asking God to forgive an attitude I had shown the night before. I was truly sorry and repented of my un-Christlike reaction to another person. As I walked down to the beach to read my Bible, I asked God to give me what I needed from Him. And as I was reading in Matthew 3, He showed me so clearly, "Therefore bring forth fruit in keeping with your repentance" (3:8, NASB). God firmly was saying to me, "Evelyn, do deeds—don't just repent in prayer!"

The word *repent* in Greek literally means to change one's mind and to turn *from* sin and *to* God. As Jesus told the woman taken in adultery to "go, and sin no more" (John 8:11), it means a drastic turnabout in thinking and lifestyle.

This expected, drastic change in actions applies to both the Christian and the non-Christian when they repent—the Christian reestablishing a God-pleasing lifestyle and the non-Christian embarking on one. Second Corinthians 7:8–10 shows us the Christian turning *back to* God, and Acts 26:20 shows the unbeliever turning *to* God.

There is a striking contrast in behavior when there is true repentance. A lifestyle just the opposite of the old one of sin emerges. Repentance produces real changes in behavior. The contrast is clearly described in Romans 6:12, 13, "Therefore do not let sin reign in your mortal body that you should obey its lusts, and do not go on presenting the members of your body to sin as instruments of unrighteousness; *but* present yourselves to God as those alive from the dead, and your members as instruments of righteousness to God" (NASB). Repentance demands action. Don't just repent and repent. Get up from your knees and do something about it!

As I shared with my secretary the phone call from the bewildered wife whose husband was daily seeking forgiveness for sleeping with another woman, she said, "Wait until you hear this one. A call I just took was for prayer from a woman whose pastor-husband was sleeping all night, every night, with another woman; then coming home to the parsonage every morning, taking a shower, putting on clean clothes, and then going to work at the church." I wondered aloud if that pastor had ever read 2 Corinthians 6:3, "Giving no cause for offense in anything, in order that the ministry be not discredited" (NASB).

Yes, God's Word tells us that true repentance is being truly sorrowful for the sin, actively turning away from that sin, and bringing "forth fruit in keeping with repentance." Not just the big, brazen sins, but all sins! Oh, how far from this we have fallen in our modern-day understanding and handling of sin.

As you prayed the closing prayer on God's requirements at the end of the last chapter, did you pray a quickie "forgive me" prayer? If you did, were you really sorry for that sin? Did you really abhor it—enough to make you turn away from it? Or are you already back thinking about it, or perhaps even doing it? If so, you did not repent.

Why Repent?

Why repent? Because I've seen myself as God sees me.

Seeing ourselves as God sees us reveals our need to repent. This came forcefully to me when we first arrived at the cottage after Chris had surgery in 1982. Completely exhausted and frazzled, I had dashed from my last speaking engagement at a convention to drive our car, with our boat in tow, to our vacation spot. I struggled hour after hour, pushing harder and harder to catch the car ferry we were to take across Lake Michigan.

My husband, propped up on foam pillows next to me in the car, kept giving me every little direction for slowing down, turning, speeding up, and parking. I found myself getting more and more edgy, responding with short and sometimes rather unkind answers. Our son and my husband's sister were along, and I suddenly became aware of how I must look in their eyes—and was not at all pleased.

However, the very next day as I took my Bible down to the beach for my early morning devotions, I saw something much more important than how they saw me. I was reading in the first chapter of 2 Peter, carefully observing the wonderful list of Christian attributes. While reading "applying all diligence, in your faith supply moral excellence, . . . godliness; . . . brotherly kindness, . . . Christian love" (1:5–7, NASB), suddenly, the word *kindness* almost jumped out at me.

Then these words in the next two verses horrified me: "If these qualities are yours and are increasing, they render you neither useless nor unfruitful in the true knowledge of our Lord Jesus Christ. For he who lacks these qualities is blind or shortsighted, . . . for as long as you practice these things, you will never stumble" (2 Pet. 1:8–10, NASB).

Suddenly, I saw myself as God saw me. Oh, how much more important this was than how other people saw me— even those dear to me! Weeping, I repented there alone on the deserted beach.

Peter must have felt like this when, after he had denied Jesus three times following His arrest, the Lord turned and looked at him. Peter, too, must have seen himself as the Son of God saw him—a deserter. The hurt that must have been in Jesus' eyes sent Peter out, weeping bitterly in deep remorse and repentance (Matt. 26:75).

In another instance, the song leader of one of our seminars shared a difficult situation which her husband, as chairman of their church, had to handle. Their pastor and his secretary were having an affair. The board kept the matter just within the board; and, after the pastor had confessed his sin and was deeply repentant, they sent him to a Christian counseling center for psychological restoration because they felt he needed the help. However, they knew his usefulness in *that* church was over. But he, forgiven by God and the church board, is now pastoring another church.

However, the secretary's reaction was not the same. To this day, she has not seen, or at least admitted, that what she did was sin. The church board, of course, fired her. She now has a job in another church but constantly complains that she just isn't accepted any more, and people don't seem to like her.

How does God see a woman like this? As a "Potiphar wife." When we read in the Bible how the wife of Potiphar repeatedly attempted to seduce God-fearing Joseph, we become incensed at her. But what is our attitude toward the modern-day "Potiphar wives" in our neighborhoods, places of employment, and, yes, even in our churches? Do we see them as God sees them? And do they see themselves as God sees them?

And the one being seduced? How many who are enjoying the flattery, attention, the ego trip, and sexual stimulation from such a person actually see her as God sees her? What would happen to our moral standards if, every time there was a seduction to any degree, we would cry out as Joseph did, "How then could I do this great evil, and sin against God?" (Gen. 39:9, NASB). Joseph saw himself as God saw him. Do we?

Somehow, we feel that if we can deceive those around us, no one will know of our sin. Also, we think we can fool those against whom we are sinning, although this usually is not true either. However, we never deceive God. David, before praying his famous "search me, O God" at the close of Psalm 139, opens it with "O Lord, Thou hast searched me and known me. . . . Even before there is a word on my tongue, Behold, O Lord, Thou dost know it all" (vv. 1–4, NASB). The writer of Hebrews expresses the same thought, "And there is no creature hidden from His sight, but all things are open and laid bare to the eyes of Him with whom we have to do" (Heb. 4:13, NASB).

Denial of our sin sometimes is a protective shield we build around ourselves to keep from getting hurt. In the self-protection of the denial, we justify the self-preservation instead of seeing the denial as God sees it—as sin. But denial actually produces the sin of "deceit," found in so many lists of sins in the Bible. Denial, of course, is lying (itself a biblical sin). Then one lie demands another, and then another, to keep covering up the original lie—until there is a hopeless web of deceit which we have spun around ourselves.

When we stop denying and start admitting to ourselves that what we are doing or have done is sin, then we are able to admit it to others—who most likely knew it anyway—and to God—who positively did know it anyway. Paul was addressing Christians when he wrote, "Do not be deceived, God is not mocked; for whatever a man sows, this he will also reap. For the one who sows to his own flesh shall from the flesh reap corruption, but the one who sows to the Spirit shall from the Spirit reap eternal life" (Gal. 6:7–8, NASB).

Why Repent? More Reasons

These verses in Galatians also give us one more reason for repenting—*the consequences* if we don't. Romans 2:4–6 contains frightening words about this, "Or do you think lightly of the riches of His kindness and forbearance and patience, not knowing that the kindness of God leads you to repentance? But because of your stubbornness and unrepentant heart you are storing up wrath for yourself in the day of wrath and revelation of the righteous judgment of God, who will render to every man according to his deeds" (NASB).

Then Paul, addressing the people in Athens who were not Christians, used these clear words, "Therefore having overlooked the times of ignorance, God is now declaring to men that all everywhere should repent, because He has fixed a day in which He will judge the world in righteousness" (Acts 17:30–31, NASB).

God does not ask, "Would you like to repent?" or say, "It would be nice if you did." No, rather, He is saying in His word that we must repent—or else face His consequences.

Another surprising reason for repenting is found in Psalm 38:3—David's prayer as a suffering penitent, "There is no *health* in my bones because of my sin" (NASB). And he goes on to describe his physical problems that he is suffering because of God's indignation. James echoes this same thought in his epistle, chapter 5, verses 14–16, where he links the confession of sins one to another and prayer for one another—so that there may be healing.

This is illustrated in the life of a pastor, who was afflicted with many physical problems. Crying out in anguish over a personal sin in which he had been living, he asked, "God, are You punishing me?" God answered by showing this pastor from Psalm 32:3, 4 that, by living in his sin while he preached for several years, he had broken God's moral laws. "When I kept silent about my sin, my body wasted away," lamented the pastor with the Psalmist.

In effect, God was answering, "I have decreed My moral

law from before the foundation of the world. My answer is already recorded in My holy Word. You are reaping the already known results of breaking My moral law."

But how wonderful that God added verse 5, "I acknowledged my sin to Thee, And my iniquity I did not hide; I said, 'I will confess my transgressions to the Lord'; And Thou didst forgive the guilt of my sin" (NASB). And this pastor, with David, rejoiced at God's forgiveness when he admitted his sin and repented.

This same thought is found in Christ's message to the church in Thyatira in the Book of Revelation where the Son of God is described to this church as having "eyes like a flame of fire" (2:18, NASB). And He was seeing this church tolerating the woman Jezebel—leading His bond servants into immorality. And then He gave the *dire results* if there was no repentance (Rev. 2:18–22).

In fact, all but two of the seven churches given messages by the Lord in the Book of Revelation were told to repent. After commending the church at Ephesus for the good things they were doing, He told them He had something against them. They had left their first love. And, as inconsequential as this may seem to be, Jesus said, "Repent . . . or else I am coming to you, and *will remove your lampstand out of its place*" (Rev. 2:5, NASB). Unless they repented, Jesus was going to remove their church from their midst.

Source of the Temptation

While we recognize that the originator of all temptation since Adam and Eve's fall is Satan himself, we are witnessing his fresh frontal attack today. At our metropolitan prayer chain's recent brunch, it was reported to us that a Christian woman was seated next to another woman who refused a meal during a luncheon and explained that she was fasting.

"Oh, are you a Christian?"

"No," she replied angrily, "I'm fasting and praying to Satan to break up the marriages and ministries of Christian pastors by infidelity."

There was also a report of a Christian man who sat beside a person on a plane who had refused a meal. He was also asked if he was a Christian. He replied, "No, I'm fasting and praying to Satan to bring other men into the lives of the spouses of Christian pastors."

My prayer time this morning was interrupted by a telephone call from England. It was from a wife and mother of two children who was struggling to be the wife that God and her husband wanted her to be. "But," she wept, "although he has been a fine Christian, he is leaving tomorrow for America, is getting a divorce, and planning to marry another woman." I find myself getting very angry at this kind of sin.

Repentance Produces Revival

What do you think God answers when you as a Christian pray, "Lord, send revival"? Surprisingly, He doesn't send showers of blessings or bring others to Himself as Savior and Lord, but He first tells *us* to repent. Then the outcome of our being revived will be that others will find Christ.

Our National Prayer Committee discovered firsthand what history tells us about every revival. We were burdened for revival in our nation and had our first national meeting to pray for it in November 1982, in Washington, D.C. But we were in for a surprise. After calling prayer leaders from across the United States to participate, thinking we would be praying for *revival*, as it turned out, we spent the first half of the convention *repenting* for ourselves.

I was to bring a message on the cleansed life first; but, as our committee met the day before the conference, I knew we needed to know the reason for praying through the cleansed life. So we asked Joy Dawson, of Youth with a Mission, to speak on what revival really is. Joy asked us two questions: "What is revival?" and "Now that you know what it is, do you really want it?"

Here is her definition: "Revival is the sovereign outpouring of the Holy Spirit in God's way and in God's time *first of all upon God's people,* where the revelation of God's holiness is greatly amplified and, as a result, God's viewpoint of sin is revealed. . . . Revival is God greatly stirring, shaking and changing His people from apathy, selfishness and self-promotion to desperate praying, humble, open and broken people with a passion only for God Himself and His glory."

As I asked God what I should speak on after Joy Dawson's

message, He laid 2 Chronicles 7:14 heavily on my heart. I was hoping for something newer and fresher as we have almost worn out this one, using it as our "American Christian" theme verse for several years. Yet, we may have been missing its message. God said to me, "Put the emphasis on *My* emphasis of this verse." Here it is: "If *my* people, which are called by *my* name, shall humble *themselves,* and pray, and seek my face, and turn from *their* wicked ways; then will I hear from heaven, and will forgive *their* sin, and will heal their land" (emphasis mine).

We have been blaming our national problems on and pointing our fingers at humanists, abortionists, pornography kings, and atheists; but God in His Word points His finger at us— His people—and lays the responsibility squarely at our feet.

Following the message on the cleansed life, we started confessing our own sins at about 4:30 in the afternoon of that first day. With just a short break for dinner, we were back praying and weeping over the sins God was bringing to our minds until midnight. And the next day, it kept up until the afternoon. We were shocked at the seemingly inconsequential attitudes and deeds God kept expecting these national leaders to confess.

I remember being called on late in the night to come to the front to lead in prayer, but I was weeping so hard I could barely speak. Why? Because God had reproved me of previously unrecognized sin. To me, it was such a trivial thing that I had not realized it was a sin until God started reproving me. It was just a tiny speck of satisfaction, unseen, deep within me, of a competitor recognizing the scope of my ministry. "Repent first, you leaders!"

At times, we weren't too sure ourselves that we wanted revival either, but the power we felt as God finally led us to pray for others was one of the greatest joys of my life. Real revival is always characterized by true repentance. In fact, without it, there is no revival.

Evangelism Versus Revival

America is long overdue for a revival. Since early in the 1600s, we have had a revival somewhere in our country on the average of every twenty years. But in the twentieth century, we have had "brush fires" here and there, but not one major revival. We have had much evangelism, but no real revival.

What is the difference? Evangelism, while scripturally accurate and commanded, is man-initiated; but revival is strictly God-initiated. Evangelism, hopefully, is inspired and empowered by the Holy Spirit; but revival is God taking the initiative and sending His outpouring in response to extraordinary prayer.

Differing from evangelism, revival always produces repentance first in the Christians who are praying for it. Evangelism centers on the one who does not know Christ as Savior and Lord; but revival, after Christians have been revived through repentance, then results in people who do not know Christ repenting and receiving Him.

I have prayed for revival for forty years; but three years ago, I prayed for it specifically in my birthday prayer for the next year in my life. It was when the urgency of praying for revival was breaking in America that my heart was more and more burdened for this revival. Since I already knew it always started with Christians seeing God's holiness first, I prayed a two-pronged birthday prayer, "Lord, show me Your holiness—and send revival."

As I waited in the stillness of my prayer closet for His answer, He directed my thinking to that time-worn Scripture portion on holiness in Isaiah 6. As I turned to it and read, my heart almost exploded within me, just as it had that morning more than three years earlier on the beach at Lake Michigan when I recorded in my Bible, "Explosion of worship and adoration! Spontaneous! Slowly drew in my breath at *who God is.*"

Also in the margin of my Bible at Isaiah 6:1–4 were the words I had recorded the year before at Deerfield Beach in Florida, "At Isaiah's words, 'lofty and exalted,' tears popped into my eyes. I shut my eyes and lifted my face to the morning sun—streaming in through the deck's open window with ocean roaring below. The tears slowly trickled down my cheeks as my heart soared up to Him—lofty and exalted. Oh," I continued writing, "how weak those English words are. What must God *really* be? There are no words! Only—'Holy, holy, holy.' "

No words ever did come for my prayer that morning in

Florida. I was just engulfed, enwrapped by who God is. Soaking into my whole being—just like the sun warming my body—was God. Holy!

Again, on that birthday morning, I saw His unique, awesome purity. I saw with Isaiah the seraphim above Him, calling to one another the only attribute of God recorded in triplicate, "Holy, holy, holy!" (Isa. 6:3). I had glimpsed a speck of His holiness!

But at this birthday time, I had asked for more—revival also. And when I saw His holiness, I cried with Isaiah, "Woe is me" (Isa. 6:5). All I, too, could see was my sinfulness, my unworthiness to be in His holy presence. For two weeks, it continued as I was letting God search me and cleanse me—preparing *me* for revival.

So, when Christians earnestly start praying for revival, God always shows them His holiness and answers them with, "You must repent first!"

Recently, I was asked to conduct a noon staff prayer meeting of a large Christian television organization. They were to begin eight days of revival on their campus in a few days and asked me to lead them in preparatory prayer for it. Defining the difference between revival and evangelism, I then talked about seeing God's holiness and seeing ourselves as Isaiah did—as sinners.

Before confessing aloud our sins, I asked how many of them who had just lifted their hands as we sang songs of praise had actually lifted up hands full of sin. Hands that had turned the pages of a pornographic magazine, dialed to an X-rated TV movie, touched forbidden fruit—when the Bible says explicitly that we are to hold up *"holy* hands" (1 Tim. 2:8). Shocked, many of them wept as they prayed for forgiveness.

Forgiven!

Since there are two classes of sin—the singular state of sin into which all humans are born and the plural sins that we commit after we become Christians—there are also two classes of repentance. And God's Word calls on both categories of sinners to repent.

What happens when we have gone through the steps of admitting to God that we have sinned, God has answered that we must repent, and we have truly repented? What then?

It is like the missionary surgeon in Ethiopia who invited my husband and me to watch an operation. The surgeon adjusted a coat hanger so that the lamp it supported focused on the abdomen of a tiny, frail woman lying on the makeshift operating table, a woman whose family had discarded her on a trash heap to die. As the surgeon tenderly reached into the gaping cavity, he scooped out a huge tumor with both hands. Looking around the tiny, ill-equipped room, he muttered, "Where'll I put this thing?" Then, stepping over to me, he said, "Here." I recoiled as he thrust that football-sized, cancerous tumor into my reluctant, bare hands.

How like that surgeon God is. A year ago, I had a particularly trying day, releasing the wounds of many years with a person who had hurt me deeply. Weeping, I afterward slumped into a chair. I was filled with self-pity and physical and emotional exhaustion. The next morning at prayer, I repented of my human reaction and asked God to remove all my un-Christlike attitudes. And suddenly, it felt as if His holy, loving hands were reaching down inside me, scooping out my cancerous attitudes.

No, God doesn't leave us on the trash heap to suffer and die when we sin. He says, "Repent!" And when we do and ask Him to forgive us, He gently yet firmly reaches down into our hearts. Then, sliding His holy hands underneath our cancerous sin, as did that surgeon at the operating table, He lifts it out completely!

When we truly repent and turn from the sin we have confessed, God answers by pulling aside the curtain; and we find ourselves stepping into a beautiful condition called *"forgiven!"*

Closing Prayer

Oh, God, I realize that my "quickie," "I-admit-I-have-sinned" prayers are not enough. I now truly repent of my sins. I abhor them, Father. I'm so sorry. And, dear Lord, I realize that my real repenting includes my turning completely away from committing these sins again. Since I have done my part, thank You for doing Your part in forgiving me.

In Jesus' name, **Amen.**

7

Be Reconciled to Me

When we pray, "I have sinned," God not only answers, "Repent," but He also includes in His answer, "Be reconciled to Me."

Reconciliation is necessary only because a relationship has been broken. And all human sin breaks the relationship between God and the one who has sinned.

While this reconciliation to God actually comes simultaneously with true repentance and forgiveness, there are two sides to the transaction. Repentance is man's action; reconciliation to God is God's action. So this is why God's forgiveness as we repent must include our reconciliation to Him.

Only when there have been broken vows, shattered commitments, or violated persons do we need to be reconciled. It is a necessity when someone is grieved, wounded, angry—or all three.

The night before a seminar, I was having dinner in a parsonage with my hostess, the minister's wife, when the phone rang. She walked to the phone and started to greet an obviously good friend, but she stopped midword. The apparently rapid-firing voice on the other end kept clipping off her responses, limiting them to "No," "Really?" "What?" My hostess's expression kept swinging from one of surprise, to a twisted grin, then to wide-eyed shock, and finally exploded into an incredible, "You didn't!"

It seems the caller had known all about her husband's girlfriend and was calling to tell the pastor's wife what she had just done. Her husband, she exploded, had just bought two new Cadillac cars—one for himself and one for his girlfriend. So incensed was the wife that she jumped into her husband's shiny new car, drove furiously to the girlfriend's house, took careful aim at the shiny new Cadillac in her driveway, slammed the gas pedal to the floor—and smashed them both.

The pastor's wife sank trembling in her chair in a state of shock. As the reality and magnitude of the deed unfolded, our responses vacillated between "Oh, no," and "That's illegal"; then, "She shouldn't have—but I don't blame her"; and finally, with the wry smile we were unable to control, we exclaimed, "Good for her!"

Who could honestly blame the wife for such uncontrolled anger? Hadn't her marriage vows, rights, and very person been violated? I inwardly breathed a sigh of relief that, if there were to be a jury, I would not have to be on it.

"Who's Angry?"

Since reconciliation is necessary only when there is enmity and hostility between people or groups, we must ask, "Who's angry?" The surprising answer is "God!"

Why does God insist on reconciliation? Because He, too, is angry at our sinning.

The Bible never speaks of God being reconciled to man, only of people being reconciled to God. Although people are frequently angry with God, He never has to be reconciled to us because we are angry. God never sins or errs in His relationship with us, thus necessitating reconciliation back to us. Only we sin against Him.

I once heard a pastor ask his Sunday school class, "Are we still, as in Jonathan Edwards's day, 'sinners in the hands of an angry God'?" Somehow this biblical view of God has been neglected or rationalized away in recent years. But the preaching of this unpopular truth by that spiritual giant in the 1700s precipitated the Great Awakening in the early years of our country. And that revival changed the course of American history. Yes, God still demands that we be reconciled to Him because He was, and still is, angry with those who sin.

God was so grieved and angry at sin that He was ready to blot out all mankind from the earth—with the exception of righteous Noah (Gen. 6:5–8). Also, God was angry with the sinning children of Israel as Moses led them toward the Promised Land for forty years. And, because of their sin, God did not permit them to enter that land (Heb. 3:17). David, too, knew all about God's wrath when He cried in Psalm 6:1, "O Lord, do not rebuke me in Thine anger, Nor chasten me in Thy wrath" (NASB).

The same truth is carried over into New Testament teaching. John the Baptist, almost echoing Jesus' words to Nicodemus in John 3:18, explained to his disciples that "he who believes in the Son has eternal life; but he who does not obey the Son shall not see life, but the wrath of God abides on him" (John 3:36, NASB).

Then after the death of Christ, Paul in Romans 1:18 warns, "For the wrath of God is revealed from heaven against all ungodliness and unrighteousness of men" (NASB). And again, "What shall we say? The God who inflicts wrath is not unrighteous, is He?" (3:5, NASB). Then Paul says to us, "Because of your stubbornness and unrepentant heart you are storing up wrath for yourself in the day of wrath and revelation of the righteous judgment of God" (Rom. 2:5, NASB).

Again, I was at a dinner the night before a seminar where a fine young woman told me her story. Although she had been deeply into the drug scene, she had wanted cassette tapes of the Bible. Her hippie friends later chided her, saying, "What are you listening to *that* for?" And she, high on drugs, would giggle and say flippantly, "Oh, it's just the Bible!"

But one day while taking a drag on a joint of marijuana, she heard on the tape, "It is a fearful thing to fall into the hands of the living God" (Heb. 10:31).

"Oh," she cried out in fright, "I don't want that to happen to me!" And she immediately accepted Christ.

Why Is God Angry?

God is angry because His holiness has been violated by our human sinning. Holiness? Yes—the attribute of God which is His own moral purity. This is not just the absence of sin in Him, but it is that God is the source and the standard of moral purity. So God not only is repulsed by our sin, He recoils in horror at it.

Yes, holiness is the only attribute of God given in triplicate in the Bible. We never read of Him as "love, love, love" or "truth, truth, truth"; but the seraphim that Isaiah saw standing above God's throne were calling to one another: "Holy, holy, holy, is the LORD of hosts" (Isa. 6:3).

So real repenting must include knowing what we have done, not only to the other people involved, but to God. We must realize that in sinning we have violated His holiness, thus causing His anger. And it is only through our repenting and His forgiving that reconciliation between Him and us can take place.

With Whom Is God Angry?

Since there are two classes of sin, there are two classes of sinners with whom God is angry. Thus, there are two categories of sinners who need to repent and be reconciled to God— reconciled to Him either for *the first time* or *back* to Him.

The first class of sin is that state of sin into which all humans are born.

Paul in Romans 5:18 told us why we are already judged while explaining how all have sinned through the sin of Adam and Eve: "So then as through one transgression there resulted condemnation to all men" (NASB). Then he so clearly shows us the process of reconciliation to God in Romans 5:8–11:

> But God demonstrates His own love toward us, in that while we were yet sinners, Christ died for us. Much more then, having now been justified by His blood, we shall be saved from the *wrath of God* through Him. For if while we were enemies, we were reconciled to God through the death of His Son, much more, having been reconciled, we shall be saved by His life. And not only this, but we also exult in God through our Lord Jesus Christ, through whom we have now received the reconciliation (NASB).

So, since we all were born in a state of sin, if Jesus' blood has not cleansed us at salvation, we are still living in that state of sin under the wrath of God. And we still need to be reconciled to Him.

When we pray, accepting Christ as Savior, we must first recognize that we need to be reconciled to God and repent before Him because He is angry that His holiness has been violated. Jesus said it so bluntly in Luke 13:3 and 5, "Unless you repent, you will all likewise perish" (NASB), and in John 3:18, "He who does not believe has been judged already" (NASB).

This class of sinners is made up of those who are either deliberately refusing salvation in Jesus, those who are just indifferent not realizing they are lost without believing in Him, or those of the hidden mission field in our churches who are trusting in church membership but never have had a personal relationship with Jesus.

A member of our church in Rockford was one of our neighborhood Bible study teachers. She astounded us one Sunday by announcing that she had discovered during her own Bible study that she really did not know Jesus. "After twenty-nine years of prenatal care," she said, "I was born."

In my prayer seminars after reading my list of twenty-three scriptural sins and questions, which include "Are you a fake, just pretending to be a real Christian?" God powerfully breaks down cultural inhibitions, reservations, and their "we never do it that way" excuses. Sometimes, everyone just seems to explode, all praying aloud in their groups at once; and at other times, they continue one by one all over the room, as they did once for twelve minutes in Bristol, England. In a recent seminar of twenty-seven hundred people, it sounded as if two-thirds prayed aloud simultaneously, making sure they had a personal relationship with Jesus.

It is likely that some of those praying may already be real Christians but are just not sure about their personal relationship with Jesus. The Bible tells us we can be sure. With a prayer of repentance and by accepting Jesus, we can join the ranks of those assured of their reconciliation with God from that state of sin into which we were all born, "These things I have written to you who believe in the name of the Son of God, in order that you may *know* that you have eternal life" (1 John 5:13, NASB).

In Australia in 1980, almost all those attending my prayer seminars were already members of a large Bible study movement, yet never less than 25 percent of these people prayed aloud making sure they knew Jesus as Savior and Lord. As I left, the leaders of the international Bible study organization said to me, "The most important thing you taught us as Bible study authors and leaders is that we have not included in our material an opportunity to make a personal commitment to Christ. We have just taken it for granted that all who study the Bible already are saved." And I have found that the most surprising part of all is that these people in the churches are just waiting for someone to ask them.

This morning, I received a phone call from a pastor's wife who told me that the day after I had a prayer seminar in their church a man came forward to join the church. When asked by the membership committee when he had accepted Christ as Savior and Lord, he replied, "Yesterday, in Evelyn's seminar."

In Japan, nonbelievers frequently attend Christian churches for several years as seekers, without making a commitment. But I observed after conducting several prayer seminars there that many people had come to Christ. I learned why from a missionary who said, "The reason there were so many decisions for Christ is that Evelyn laid it on the line and came right out and asked them to make a decision." Reconciled to God through Jesus! "God is now declaring to men that all everywhere should repent, because He has fixed a day in which He will judge the world in righteousness" (Acts 17:30–31, NASB).

When you ask Jesus, on the final Judgment Day, "Lord, when did I not visit You in prison, feed You, and so on?"—how will you handle it if Jesus answers, "Depart from me, ye cursed" (Matt. 25:41)? What a horrifying answer this will be for those who have only been cultural Christians, who belonged to fine churches or thought they were God's grandchildren because they had believing parents.

God's Incredible Provision

But there is another side to our God. While God's holiness demands reconciliation by a sacrifice for our sin, His love provided it!

God loved us enough to send the means of reconciliation—

His own Son, Jesus. Romans 5:8 says, "But God commendeth his love toward us, in that, while we were yet sinners, Christ died for us." Jesus was the sacrifice that satisfied the demands of God's violated holiness. And this—God's own love—has saved us from His own wrath.

Christ came not only to preach the gospel but so that there would be a gospel to be preached! "For he hath made him [Jesus] to be sin for us, who knew no sin; that we might be made the righteousness of God in him" (2 Cor. 5:21). This thought about God absolutely overwhelms me. My heart cries out, "How could He not spare His own Son but deliver Him up for us all, and then do it while we were still His enemies?"

Reconciliation is the removal of God's wrath toward man by the shedding of Jesus' blood on the cross. Through Jesus, our status with God is changed. We stand in the presence of the holy God of heaven, justified—just as if we never had sinned. And reconciled—with God's wrath toward us eradicated, erased. "Not imputing their trespasses unto them" (2 Cor. 5:19). Reconciled!

Charles Colson, in a college commencement address, put it this way: "The gospel of Jesus Christ must be the bad news of the conviction of sin before it can be the good news of redemption."

In May of 1983, while on my way to a British Broadcasting interview, I noticed that my taxi was following a bus with a large sign on the back that read, "Therefore having been justified by faith, we have peace with God through our Lord Jesus Christ" (Rom. 5:1, NASB).

After looking at it for many minutes, I suddenly realized the importance of the preposition "with." When we are justified at salvation, it isn't so much that we receive the peace *of* God but peace *with* God. Reconciled!

During the same British Isles seminar tour, I was reading my Bible in Belfast and underlined Romans 8:1, "There is therefore now no condemnation for those who are in Christ Jesus" (NASB). With tears and deep gratitude welling up within me, I prayed: "Thank You, God, that You took away my condemnation when I was nine years old!" Reconciled to God! "He who believes in the Son has eternal life; but he who does not obey the Son shall not see life, but the wrath of God abides on him" (John 3:36, NASB).

Are you sure that you have been reconciled to God by

accepting Jesus as your Savior and Lord? If not, have you ever considered that God is angry since you are still living in the state of sin into which you were born? And that He is angry because you are violating His holiness? But—have you also considered that He loves you so much that He is just waiting and longing to change His relationship with you? Be reconciled to God!

Ministry of Reconciliation

Those who are already real Christians have been given the ministry of reconciliation by God. Once we have been reconciled to God through Jesus, He immediately gives us the job of reconciling others to Him. "Therefore if any man is in Christ, he is a new creature; the old things passed away; behold, new things have come. Now all these things are from God, who reconciled *us* to Himself through Christ, and gave *us* the ministry of reconciliation" (2 Cor. 5:17–18, NASB).

For the first annual symposium of Charles Colson's Prison Fellowship in Belfast in 1983, we had chosen the theme "In Christ—Reconciliation" from 2 Corinthians 5:17–20. As I spoke, I reminded the justice officials, prison workers, ex-offenders, and international board members that we must identify what this ministry of reconciliation is. Then I explained that Paul did this with his little word *namely* in the very next verse. "Namely, that God was in Christ reconciling the world to Himself" (2 Cor. 5:19, NASB). The world—always those not of the body of Jesus.

There will always be other subsequent valid and necessary teachings, but it is this word and ministry of reconciliation given to us by God that must come first. While speaking at the symposium I reminded those present that we must see every prison inmate as condemned by God, no matter what his or her status with their country's judicial system may be— unless they have been reconciled to God through faith in Christ. Even if pardoned, paroled, or freed from prison, they are still condemned to death by God unless they are reconciled to Him.

At our last U.S.A. Prison Fellowship board meeting, we reemphasized the importance of all our material stating, and members of the field staff recognizing, that real rehabilitation begins in the prisoner only when he or she has been reconciled to God through Jesus. All other teaching is subsequent to this.

On a blustery March morning during my devotions, I was "praying through" God's removing of all sin from me. Then, knowing He never leaves me as a fragile, empty shell from which He has removed these sins but that He then fills me, I started to tell Him all the things I knew I needed from Him. But suddenly, I changed my mind. "No, Lord, not what I think I need. This morning, would You please fill me with what's burdening You? Lord, what is Your number one priority for me today?" And immediately, before my mind's eye were two huge words, almost as if written in capital letters: WIN SOULS!

I often question why we spend so much time in our church prayer meetings praying for sick Christians who, if they die— and they will eventually—will go to be with Jesus; and we spend almost no time praying for the sinners who, when they die, will go to a Christless eternity.

Speaking at the Wednesday night prayer meeting in a famous church known for its deep spirituality, I mentioned in passing the appalling content of our church prayer lists. When the time came for group prayer, the interim pastor stood, holding a stack of mimeographed church prayer sheets in his hands. Then, blushing, he stammered, "I'm ashamed to hand these out." And for good reason. All but one request was for sick people. Please don't stop praying for your sick members but *add* all those who are dying without Christ—lost—unreconciled to God.

God, in giving us the ministry of reconciliation, has made us ambassadors for Christ. It is "as though God were entreating *through* us; we beg you on behalf of Christ, be reconciled to God" (2 Cor. 5:20, NASB).

In the apostle Paul's day, ambassadors were envoys responsible for bringing vanquished people into the family of the Roman Empire. Today, the Christian ambassador for Christ brings God's terms to others whereby they can become citizens of His kingdom and members of His family. Also, the honor of the Roman Empire was in the ambassador's hands; and today, the honor of Christ is in our hands. And by our lives, we cause people to think more—or less—of Christ as we seek to bring them into God's family. To have the honor of Christ and the church in our hands is a tremendous privilege but also an almost terrifying responsibility.

I learned the privilege—and responsibility—of being an ambassador for Christ during my last British Isles tour. With whole days of interviews with the secular press, before each one I prayed, "Oh, God, only let them see Jesus in me."

"The press is waiting for you in the bar." I cringed. Everything inside me rebelled as I heard the Belfast hotel clerk's words. On my one day to get over jetlag and after a four-hour picture-taking tour of the riot-torn part of Belfast, I was exhausted. Pictures in front of graffiti walls, pictures with soldiers, pictures with the mother of the first young man murdered in the Irish war—all out in the cold, windy rain—left me wanting only a bowl of hot soup and a bed. Was this what the Bible meant by being an ambassador for Christ? I gritted my teeth and breathed a desperate prayer as I marched in to meet them. "Oh, Lord, may they only see Jesus in me!"

The last interview that day was by a woman reporter who wiped away tears as she struggled to concentrate on her interviewing. Our press agent had whispered to me, "She learned just two days ago that her brother, an international rugby player, has cancer. The doctors have given him two weeks to live." Her questions turned to the ones we all ask at such times. Questions about God, eternity, healing. I longed to pray with her right then, but I knew she was not ready for that yet. I squeezed her hands in mine as I asked, "Would you like me to pray for you when I get back to my room?" Tears spilled over on her note pad as she gratefully accepted my offer.

The next week when I arrived in Birmingham, England, and was facing another one of those whole days with the secular press, I expanded my prayer: "Oh, God, keep me a pure, Christlike ambassador, only saying Your words and radiating Christ—His reactions, His love, tolerance, patience, joys, His burden for the world."

As the four to eight hours of newspaper, radio, and TV interviews, and phone-in programs every day between seminars stretched into a month, I began seeing an amazing pattern. Not one derogatory, unkind, or embarrassing question was being asked. Not one unanswerable question about President Reagan's position on the nuclear arms race. Then questions like "Isn't Reagan embarrassed that you Americans think he needs prayer?" and "Could we pray for Margaret Thatcher that way?" began to surface. Eagerness to learn more about what I believed began filling the interviews. The media people were hungry for the Jesus they saw in me.

Then, at the committee's preprayer meeting the night before one of our last seminars, an ecstatic press reporter almost exploded with the news. "That Belfast reporter accepted Christ the day after your interview, and the doctors found her brother's cancer miraculously gone!" An ambassador for Christ! The position to which God calls all who have been reconciled to Him. A reconciler. The privilege—and the responsibility.

This responsibility is explained by Paul. Immediately after the call to be ambassadors, he gives the conduct expected of one charged with the ministry of reconciliation, "And working together with Him, . . . giving no cause for offense in anything, in order that the ministry be not discredited, but in everything commending ourselves as servants of God" (2 Cor. 6:1–4, NASB).

The specific examples of the awesome lifestyle expectations for an ambassador who is reconciling the world to God goes on:

In much endurance, in afflictions, in hardships, in distresses, in beatings, in imprisonments, in tumults, in labors, in sleeplessness, in hunger, in purity, in knowledge, in patience, in kindness, in the Holy Spirit, in genuine love, in the word of truth, in the power of God; by the weapons of righteousness for the right hand and the left, by glory and dishonor, by evil report and good report; regarded as deceivers and yet true; as unknown yet well-known, as dying yet behold, we live; as punished yet not put to death, as sorrowful yet always rejoicing, as poor yet making many rich, as having nothing yet possessing all things (2 Cor. 6:4–10, NASB).

While God is calling us to be reconcilers, He at times must say to us that we have to be reconciled back to Him ourselves. Anything that gives cause for offense in our ministry is sin in God's eyes. As Christians reconciling others to God, we must be alert for anything in our lives that God considers sin.

The second class of sin is the sins that Christians commit. They are "sins," not the singular state of sin into which we all were born. These are committed after the original reconciliation with God at salvation. And this sinning also requires reconciliation with God—because He is also angry at our sinning as Christians.

Why shouldn't God be angry? After all, He has entrusted to us the honor of our Christ and of our church, but our sin has made a mockery of the sinless Christ we are representing as ambassadors.

After we are washed clean by repenting and accepting Jesus as Savior and Lord—reconciled to God—we still create enmity between Him and ourselves when we sin. This does not mean that we have broken our initial relationship of reconciliation to Him obtained at salvation, but we have created a gulf between God and ourselves by our sins. Our sinning has broken our formerly established communication and fellowship with God. Thus, reconciliation is necessary.

Peter, writing to Christians, said it so well in his first epistle, "The eyes of the Lord are upon the righteous, and His ears attend to their prayer, but the face of the Lord is against those who do evil" (1 Peter 3:12, NASB).

The apostle John, writing to Christians, tells us that "the blood of Jesus keeps on cleansing us from all sin"—if we confess it. And then "[God] is faithful and righteous to forgive *us* our sins and to cleanse *us* [not those still in their original state of sin] from all unrighteousness" (1 John 1:9, NASB).

So again we ask, who's angry? God! It is not important that we may be angry at God but that God is angry with us. Even as Christians, we can violate His holiness over and over again.

In Romans, chapter 1, God gives a sickening picture of the sins of those He finally gave over to a depraved mind—women and men exchanging "the natural function for that which is unnatural" (v. 26, NASB), full of "all unrighteousness, wickedness, greed, malice; full of envy, murder, strife, deceit, malice; they are gossips, slanderers, haters of God, insolent, arrogant, boastful, inventors of evil, disobedient to parents, without understanding, untrustworthy, unloving, unmerciful" (vv. 29–31, NASB). But in chapter 2, he switches from the world's sins and directly addresses the Christians to whom he is writing. Paul says this to them:

Therefore *you* are without excuse, every man *of you* who passes judgment, for in that you judge another, you condemn yourself; for you who judge practice the same things. And we know that the judgment of God rightly falls upon those who practice such things. And do you suppose this, O man, when you pass judgment upon those who practice such things and do the same yourself, that you will escape the judgment of God? . . . But because of your stubbornness and unrepentant heart *you* are storing up wrath for yourself in the day of wrath and revelation of the righteous judgment of God, who will render to every man according to his deeds (vv. 1–3, 5, 6, NASB).

With what sins of Christians is God angry? All of them! Paul explained to the Christians in Colossae: "Therefore consider the members of your earthly body as dead to immorality, impurity, passion, evil desire, and greed, which amounts to idolatry. For it is on account of these things that the *wrath of God* will come" (Col. 3:5–6, NASB). Not on the sin but on the sinner. God doesn't punish sin, He punishes the sinners.

While a pastor's wife, I remember walking into our empty church time and time again and finding one of the members, who had deserted his wife and child for another woman, grieving in the darkened sanctuary. Holding his head in his hands, he would shudder repeatedly, not only over what he had done to his family but at what he had done to God. He had violated God's holiness.

What an awesome thought this is to me. All of my sins violate God's holiness! Me, His child! All of my pride, touchiness, unkindness, anxiety, lack of faith—the list seems so endless—violate my heavenly Father's holiness!

The Bible contains many lists of sins God's children are to avoid. Jesus' list in Mark 7:21–22 covers a large number of the glossed-over "common" sins Christians commit as well as those horrible ones found *even* in our families and churches. Scripture is God's source of reproof for us. "Oh that my ways may be established / To keep Thy statutes! / Then I shall not be ashamed / When I look upon all Thy commandments" (Ps. 119:5–6, NASB).

As I read this, my heart cried out with the Psalmist, "Oh, to come to the place where I need no reproof from the Scripture and am not ashamed when I look in it—because I am keeping all His statutes!"

His Holy Presence

So few people, Christians and non-Christians, are even aware that they are not reconciled to God. It comes as a complete shock that while they are living in sin, although He still loves them, God certainly doesn't like them.

When I feel far from God and pray, "Father, I long for a deeper, closer walk with You," God answers me with "My child, you have broken our fellowship with your sin. You must be reconciled to Me first."

When my efforts as a reconciler of the world to God are ineffective and in frustration I ask God why, He frequently insists, "You must be reconciled to Me first!"

When I pray, "Lord, give me power in prayer," He sometimes answers literally, "Since you are regarding iniquity in your heart, I cannot hear you" (see Ps. 66:18). "Repent and let Me reconcile you once again to Myself—and reestablish our powerful relationship."

The only reason God convicts us of sin and demands repentance is so that we can be reconciled to Him and once again experience fellowship with Him. It is so that we can step into that room marked *His holy presence.* "Who may ascend into the hill of the LORD? And who may stand in His holy place? He who has clean hands and a pure heart" (Ps. 24:3–4, NASB).

Yes, when we have sinned, our part is to repent—and God's part is to reconcile us to Himself.

When God answers, "I forgive you and have reconciled you back to Myself," we step into the rare privilege of being, uninhibited and unrestrained, in the very presence of the holy God of the universe. All hindrances to His presence are swept away, and we walk hand in hand with Him—just as if we never had sinned! "Yet He has now reconciled you in His fleshly body through death, in order to present you before Him holy and blameless and beyond reproach" (Col. 1:22, NASB).

Closing Prayer

Oh, God, I confess that I have violated Your holiness and, thus, our relationship is broken. Please, God, cleanse me from all known and unknown sin. And thank You, Father, for being holy enough to be angry at my sin—but loving enough to forgive me and to reconcile me to Yourself.

In Jesus' name, **Amen.**

8

WHEN GOD ANSWERS . . .

Be Reconciled to Others

Complete reconciliation to God is not possible without a willingness to be reconciled to others as well. Why? Because one of the clear commands in the Bible is that we be reconciled to others. And as long as we are not obeying God's scriptural commands, we are sinning—and thus not reconciled to Him. "If someone says, 'I love God,' and hates his brother, he is a liar; for the one who does not love his brother whom he has seen, cannot love God whom he has not seen" (1 John 4:20, NASB).

Frequently, I am asked, "Do you mean you pray with *them?*" Aghast, they are wondering aloud how I could stoop to, and even defile myself by, praying together with Christians of different denominations or forms of worship.

At the International Prayer Assembly in Seoul, Korea, in June 1984, I was asked to be on the committee writing the "International Call to Prayer" for the sponsoring Lausanne Committee on World Evangelization. While discussing which Christians around the world we should call to prayer, the representative of a European country said, "If we include *them,* those praying in my country will throw this out."

Acting as secretary for this section, I became exasperated and inwardly horrified at such a discussion. Finally, facetiously yet firmly, I asked, "As I word this for the printer, should I include all those with whom we are going to spend eternity in heaven, or. . . ." There was a long, shocked silence. Then all agreed with emphatic oneness that world-wide prayer is for *all* Christians. Blushing in shame, the European delegate apologized profusely. "Therefore I want the men [people] in every place to pray, lifting up holy hands, *without wrath and dissension*" (1 Tim. 2:8, NASB).

Although we are carnivorous beings, one thing that distinguishes us from most other meat-eating creatures is that we do not devour one another. However, there are times when this is not true in the body of Christ.

I can recall more than ten years ago when two large national organizations were vying for the potential prayer power of our Twin Cities. Both had fine fruit-bearing ministries, but they were almost pushing and shoving to persuade our local pray-ers to sign up with them. In the midst of the controversy, I called out to God, "Oh, Father, solve this ugly competition for me. What is Your answer?" And He shocked me with His oh-so-relevant reply from Galatians 5:15, "If you bite and devour one another, take care lest you be consumed by one another" (NASB).

No Reconciliation to God without It

At the end of His earthly life, Jesus prayed to the Father in His high-priestly prayer about this requirement that we Christians be reconciled to one another. And as long as we are not reconciled to each other, we are sinning because we are disobeying this recorded desire of Jesus. And, of course, as long as there is sin in our lives, we are not reconciled to God. Jesus prayed:

> I do not ask in behalf of these [whom the Father gave Him] alone, but for those also who believe in Me through their word; *that* they may all be one; even as Thou, Father, art in Me, and I in Thee, *that* they also may be in Us; *that* the world may believe that Thou didst send Me. And the glory which Thou hast given Me I have given to them; *that* they may be one, just as We are one; I in them, and Thou in Me, *that* they may be perfected in unity, *that* the world may know that Thou

didst send Me, and didst love them, even as Thou didst love Me (John 17:20–23, NASB, emphasis mine).

Contrary to popular thought, Jesus did not ask His children to be reconciled so that they *could become one,* but because they *were* one! So, whenever we pray asking God with which Christians we should pray, He answers, "But you *are* one!" "There is neither Jew nor Greek, there is neither slave nor free man, there is neither male nor female; for you are all one in Christ Jesus" (Gal. 3:28, NASB).

But God's requirement for reconciliation is broader than just within the body of Christ. It includes *individual* reconciliation to mates, parents, in-laws, children, brothers, sisters, pastors, neighbors, employees, employers, competitors, and our enemies—all of whom may or may not be Christians. So, as long as we are not reconciled to even one of them, we are not obeying Jesus' plan for us. "Forgiving each other, whoever has a complaint against *any one;* just as the Lord forgave you, so also should you" (Col. 3:13, NASB).

This "any one" includes *societal* reconciliation—encompassing people of every race, color, sex, denomination, political party, capital and labor, youth and the aged. First John 2:9 clearly states, "The one who says he is in the light and yet hates his brother is in the darkness until now" (NASB).

Thus, being unwilling to be reconciled to other people is a sin, which must be confessed, repented of, forgiven, and turned from if we are to be reconciled back to God.

In 1983, just before leaving war-torn Belfast for America after the Prison Fellowship's powerful International Symposium on "Reconciliation," I was interviewed on a local television station. "What is your parting word for the TV audiences in Ireland?" the interviewer asked.

Looking directly into the camera, I said, "Be reconciled. Forgive—and ask God to forgive you!"

Horrified, my sweet Christian hostess retorted, "After what *they* did?" Then she flushed with embarrassment, remembering the words of God—and the theme of our symposium: "Be ye reconciled!"

So, Who's Angry?

On a human level, it really doesn't matter who is angry. Whether we are angry with someone, or they are angry with us, or if the feeling is mutual—the answer from God is the same: "Be reconciled!"

When it was God who was angry at our sinning because we had violated His holiness, we had to be reconciled to Him. But whenever there are broken relationships here on earth, His instructions to us are equally clear: "Be reconciled to each other!"

Jesus, in Matthew 5:22–24, gives us extremely hard admonitions: "But I say to *you* that every one *who is angry with his brother* shall be guilty before the court; and whoever shall say to his brother, 'Raca,' shall be guilty before the supreme court; and whoever shall say, 'You fool,' shall be guilty enough to go into the hell of fire" (NASB).

Then Jesus looks at the other side—anger against you. "If therefore you are presenting your offering at the altar, and there remember that *your brother has something against you,* leave your offering there before the altar, and go your way; first be reconciled to your brother, and then come and present your offering" (vv. 23–24). No anger at others or by others is tolerated by Jesus.

How Is Reconciliation Possible?

In this world of such diverse desires, goals, and dogmas, is it realistic to believe the real body of Christ can be reconciled? As members of the human race, our answer has to be "No, it never can work." However, this answer is wrong because the reconciliation has already been accomplished on the cross of Christ.

Jesus *was* the answer to this question. Paul tells us in Ephesians 2 that the blood of Christ broke down the dividing wall between the Gentiles and the Jews of the Old Testament, "Who made both groups into one, . . . that in Himself He . . . might *reconcile them both in one body* to God through the cross, by it having put to death the enmity" (vv. 14–16, NASB).

He also tells us that those who were united in the body of Christ "have put on the new self who is being renewed . . . a renewal in which there is no distinction between Greek and Jew, circumcised and uncircumcised, barbarian, Scythian, slave and freeman, but Christ is all, and in all" (Col. 3:10–

11, NASB). Therefore, our responsibility is to live out in our daily lives what has already been accomplished for us by Jesus. Reconciliation is the application of Christ's work on the cross.

Jesus Is the Answer

A letter from Charles Colson included a story which, he said, so beautifully demonstrates the reconciling power of Jesus Christ. (I have changed the names of the inmates.) He wrote:

"It is about two inmates. One is Steve, a muscular forty-year-old man currently serving a five-year sentence for his involvement in pornography. He entered prison already a tough, hot-tempered man; prison life hardened him even further, making him bitter and resentful.

"During Steve's trial the key witness against him was an older man, John, a respected member of a special task force against pornography. But four years later John himself was convicted—ironically—on a morals charge. He was sentenced to the very institution where Steve was imprisoned.

"As soon as Steve learned from the inmate grapevine that his old accuser was in prison with him, he became obsessed with finding ways to get even. It started with harassment and an attempt at blackmail. Still Steve's hatred was unsatisfied, and finally the inevitable happened: Steve let it be known he was out to kill John.

"As I can testify from my own time in prison," wrote Colson, "behind the walls there is no one more universally hated than an informant or government witness; and John, a small, frail man, feared it was only a matter of time before he would be beaten or stabbed.

"However, during the weekend of May 3–5, 1985, we conducted one of our in-prison evangelism seminars at that prison. Incredibly, both Steve and John signed up to attend. Although Steve probably viewed it as an opportunity to stalk his prey, God had other plans. After the weekend of clear teaching on the forgiveness available through Jesus Christ, instructor Lorraine Williams closed with a special challenge.

" 'If there is anyone here who needs to forgive another person, I challenge you to do something about it—right now.'

"After a minute of heavy silence, Steve stood up. Would

this be his time to strike? Or had this 'religious stuff' become too irritating for his bitter spirit to bear? No one was quite sure as he began walking toward John. Shaking, John sat with his head bowed.

"Finally, Steve stopped square in front of the man he wanted to murder. John lifted his head, and the two enemies faced each other in front of the entire seminar group.

" 'I'm sorry,' Steve said timidly. 'Will you forgive me?' Shocked, John paused a moment, then nodded slowly. 'I will,' he said, and as Steve sat down next to him, the two pledged to work out their differences as *Christian* brothers."

Not retaliation, not retribution, but reconciliation in Jesus!

Reconciliation in Prayer Seminars

In our prayer seminars through the years, we, too, have seen innumerable instances of striking reconciliations. The struggles and then the joy that bursts forth is astounding. Weeping, hugging, dashing for a phone, or turning to a friend for forgiveness or to forgive—these fill every seminar with life-changing experiences. Seeing the real body of Christ praying with and for each other during a prayer seminar is one of our great joys. We see political, cultural, racial, and personal differences resolved and the oneness of the body of Christ emerging—sometimes slowly and haltingly, but nevertheless beginning.

A scene of cultural reconciliation that moved me deeply took place in Madras, India. The committee there had wisely scheduled the prayer seminar in the gorgeous cathedral in that city, attracting many elite ladies. So they came, wearing their shimmering, pure silk sarees decorated with designs made of gold and silver threads. And the poor, some in rags, came, too. The leaders of the city told me that, with the caste system still very much a part of their culture, this was the first time these two groups had ever come together, much less repeatedly prayed together all day, holding hands in their small groups.

When the seminar was over, I had to leave for another appointment. But they did not want to go. They said they had not finished praying together. As I reluctantly walked out the front door of that huge cathedral, I turned to see—reconciliation. I caught my breath as I saw the women kneeling in circles all over the cathedral, with their foreheads touching the floor, and their sarees pulled up over their heads in a sweeping kaleidoscopic effect. A beautiful step in breaking down a centuries-old division which humans had built.

Much of this unity is the result of the ground rules we insist be followed in our seminars. First, before I accept an invitation to conduct a prayer seminar, we request that the *organizing committee* find one born-again Christian from each participating church in the community to be on the steering committee. The shocked response usually goes something like this, "You mean there is a real Christian in *that* church?" (Of course, we are careful to explain the difference between real members of the body of Christ and just church members.) Then they are pleasantly surprised to find real sisters and brothers in Christ in *all* the churches.

However, the reason for this composition of steering committees is not so much for the work that needs to be done, but to fulfill the requirement that there be concentrated prayer at their regular meetings six months prior to the seminar. Then I have the unspeakable privilege of stepping into their committee dinner and prayer meeting the night before the seminar and feeling myself surrounded by their mutual love and engulfed by their power in corporate prayer.

I tell them that after they have learned to pray together like this, they hardly need me to come for a seminar! They have already discovered, usually for the first time, the oneness of the body of Christ in their area—an absolute necessity for the large metropolitan telephone prayer chains or other joint community-wide ventures they are planning to organize after our seminar.

I shall never forget praying with the committee in Glasgow, Scotland, the night before our prayer seminar there in 1981. The committee was made up of outstanding women leaders; and, in spite of some doctrinal differences, there was a unique and powerful oneness in Christ which had grown through the months of their praying together. But that night, they had invited their husbands and pastors. Some of the women even had to get permission to pray in the presence of those men (which in some instances was rather reluctantly granted). But as we knelt to pray together, my husband and I became acutely aware of a beautiful oneness in Jesus emerging. Finally, exploding with the wonder of the presence of God there, my

Chris burst out in song, leading us all in singing on our knees, *"He* is Lord, He is Lord!" And we were all one—bound together in Him!

Another seminar rule that has produced this amazing reconciliation is to *invite all*—races, colors, denominations, political parties. One area of our country seemed almost to be still fighting the Civil War as they asked me to hold a prayer seminar. When they noted that one of the prerequisites for a seminar was that all the churches of the community had to be welcome, they said, "But never in our history have we done it that way."

"Then I don't come."

"Oh, Evelyn," lamented their godly leader, "I feel just horrible about this; but I know which of our members will get up and walk out if a black person comes to our church."

With great trepidation, but also with determined courage, this lovely woman president called on the women's leader of the neighboring black church. When she issued her invitation to come to their church, the black leader stammered, "But we aren't welcome in your church."

"I know you're not," came the chagrined reply. "But I'm inviting you anyway."

And they came. Hesitantly, cautiously, they sat there, furtively glancing from side to side to see how "they" were reacting. But before we knew it, God was at His work of reconciliation, and the age-old barriers began to melt away. Joy started taking over. By the end of the day, I wiped away tears as I watched them holding hands in prayer circles, with the love of Jesus radiating from so many of their faces. Reconciled? It surely was a start!

The problem was reversed when the auxiliary of the black ministerial association sponsored my prayer seminar in a southern state. It was an exciting time with great fellowship. And all of their pastors came, taking notes all through the day. I had a delightful time of warmth and acceptance by all—except a few women who were furious that their pastor would stoop to be taught by a white woman. But there's another invitation on my desk right now—from *these* same women!

In our recent seminars in Guam and Western Australia, a familiar pattern surfaced. For the first time, Christians of all persuasions came together to learn to pray. And in Taiwan, for the first time, both political sides came together to learn to pray with representatives from forty-three different Christian organizations and church affiliations, with the result that there are now more than ten thousand organized pray-ers from both sides on that island.

It was during our 1981 prayer seminar in Belfast, Northern Ireland, which produced so much prayer for Liam and other prisoners, that we saw amazing reconciliation. I had the audience form prayer groups of four, with a strange mixture of Protestants and Catholics—at war—in each. My Scripture Press hosts and my husband watched from a high balcony. And for the first time, for them, and for me, we witnessed actual physical trembling in prayer as people forgave someone. Forgave the ones who had bombed their home or place of business, killed or maimed their loved ones. There it was— at least a little glimmer of hope for future reconciliation.

Closing reconciliation. The last praying we do in our seminars is an active step toward reconciliation. At the close, those who have been praying together all day in groups of four are given a final assignment. I ask one group member to name his or her church and the pastor or priest. Then the one on that person's right will pray for them by name while all the other members are praying silently. As we go around our little circles, each church and pastor or priest represented in the seminar will be the recipient of intercessory prayer. Frequently, this is the first time many of them have ever prayed for another church, especially if it is considered a competitor or has even a slightly different way of worshiping God.

Then to close the prayer seminar, we all join hands across the whole auditorium—those who have had a personal relationship with Christ for years and those who just that day made sure of their membership in the real body. And we sing together:

> Blest be the tie that binds
> Our hearts in Christian love;
> The fellowship of kindred minds
> Is like to that above.[1]

---

1. From *Tabernacle Hymns Number Five,* © 1953 by Tabernacle Publishing Co., Chicago, Illinois, 1963.

Then, while they all are still holding hands, I say, "Now squeeze!" And the final burst of unity comes in this parting hand-squeeze as big smiles spread across faces—sometimes surprising even themselves. And many turn to embrace their new-found friends in Christ. Or to weep. Or both. Reconciled in the real body of Christ!

I believe God has given me a ministry of reconciliation— not only of the sinner to God, but of brother and sister to brother and sister. And it works! But I also know that this unity is one of God's astounding answers to thousands of prayers through the years for these seminars by my prayers and the local seminar committees.

Secrets of Reconciliation

There are many secrets of reconciliation that we teach and practice, but the most important one seems to be *forgive*.

I received a phone call from a woman who had been at my prayer seminar the day before, but had left without forgiving her family. As I listened over the phone to this distraught and screaming woman, it occurred to me that I was probably receiving her "suicide call." (I learned later that she actually had tried to take her own life twice before.)

"Mrs. Christenson," she screamed, "did you mean what you said Jesus said yesterday?" Asking her what it was, she literally screeched over the phone, "You said that Jesus said that if I don't forgive others now that I've become a Christian, God won't forgive me the sins I've committed as a Christian either."

Assuring her that Jesus really did say that both in Matthew 6 and Mark 11, I queried, "Why, what's wrong?"

"If you knew about my childhood," she shrieked, "you would never teach that again!" Then describing its horror, she continued, "My older brother raped me almost every night from the time I was seven. And my father, with my mother standing there consenting, would tie me to the bed and abuse my body. Then one day, he stripped me naked, tied me to a tree outside, and mutilated my body so badly that I never can have children. I'm going in for my second corrective surgery at the end of this week."

Oh, how I wanted to tell her Jesus really didn't say that and that I had just made it all up. But I could not lie. Jesus did say those words. So I kept her on the phone, talking and praying with her, striving desperately for a long time to change her mind. Then abruptly, she said, "I just bought a copy of your book *Gaining through Losing*. Will this do any good?"

Relieved at her abrupt change of attitude, I replied, "Yes. In the seminar, we only learned about your responsibility to forgive, but there is more to it than that. There is a chapter in that book about what will happen to you if you don't forgive them."

She ended the phone call by promising to read the chapter; and it was just two days later that she called back. Her happy-sounding voice exclaimed, "Well, I did it. I forgave them!" We rejoiced together, and I called the prayer chains to tell them the good news and thank them for praying.

But two days later, she called again. "Well," she announced victoriously, "I did the whole thing! My family is a thousand miles away, but I called to tell them I'd forgiven them and"— she soberly added—"to ask them to forgive my unforgiving attitude toward them."

Her pastor had been out of the country during that week, and I asked if he had returned. He, along with other professional counselors, had tried to help her for more than two years. When I asked what he had said when he saw her, she proudly reported, "Judy Rae, that's the fastest transformation I've ever seen!" Reconciled by forgiving.

Time magazine of January 9, 1984, in an article about Pope John Paul spending minutes in prison with his would-be assassin, Mehmet Ali Agca, recorded these startling words: "As Pope John Paul tenderly held the hand that had held the gun that was meant to kill him—it was a startling drama of forgiveness and reconciliation."

Isn't it amazing how the admonition in Ephesians 4:31–32 really does work? "Let all bitterness and wrath and anger and clamor and slander be put away from you, along with all malice. And be kind to one another, tender-hearted, forgiving each other, just as God in Christ also has forgiven you" (NASB).

In addition to forgiving, another secret of reconciliation is *love*. In our "What Happens When We Pray" seminars, we have practiced the scriptural reconciliation formula in 2 Corinthians 2:5–11 for years, with truly remarkable results. After forgiving someone, we ask God for all the love He wants us to have for that person, wait in prayer to feel it come, and then go home to confirm that new love.

A letter from a Nevada seminar participant shares the miracle God performed in her life:

> Dearest Evelyn:
>
> I can't tell you how much your life and message have affected mine! I lost my dear mother five years ago and she was such a godly, loving woman and mother as you are.
>
> My father remarried three years ago . . . a woman who just couldn't seem to love me. The hurt was deep and intense as she took many opportunities, where love could have been shared, to express rejection and bitter dislike . . . maybe even bordering on hate.
>
> I have prayed much about this but a root of bitterness began to develop which also spread into other relationships, making me very touchy and emotionally unstable.
>
> At your prayer seminar in Reno, Nevada, I had three people placed on my heart whom I had a lot of bitterness toward. I forgave them during the seminar (with many tears), and within the next two weeks the Lord beautifully brought about true forgiveness between all three persons and myself and also brought about opportunities for sincere and true reconciliation.
>
> I received the first letter I have ever received from my stepmother, and it was a sincere attempt to express love to me. The Lord also freed me to express love to her by allowing her to be in a great need!
>
> I can't express the freedom, joy and new fruitfulness which has come into my life because of this forgiveness and release from bitterness.
>
> Thank you so much for being the Lord's willing and anointed handmaiden. I love you so much in Him! God bless you *so much!*
>
> Tressa

The night Jesus was betrayed, He gave these words to His disciples, "A new commandment I give to you, that you love one another, . . . By this all men will know that you are My disciples, if you have love for one another" (John 13:34–35, NASB).

I watched a beautiful Christian mother whose son was deeply involved in organized crime live out this Scripture. Loving unconditionally, forgiving and forgiving again—although certainly not condoning—she kept her arms and home open to him through the years of agonized waiting and praying. How much easier it would have been for her to kick him out of her home or to disown him, as is done so frequently by embarrassed or angry parents. But it all paid off. He has come back to the Lord; and now he, his wife, and mother are living as inseparable friends.

Marriage Oneness

So often we hear, "My marriage has been over for a long time." No, this is not true. Incompatibility, cooled love, or conflicting interests do not dissolve the "one flesh" God created at the time of the marriage. What the couple needs most is reconciliation.

My autograph lines are full of people with shining eyes, joyously explaining how their marriages have been saved as they followed the instructions in our seminars or in the book, *What Happens When Women Pray,* to forgive, love, and confirm their love.

In a beautiful letter to me, a woman apologized for not telling me about her reconciliation with her husband six years ago. She said they were on the verge of divorce, fighting continuously, and were emotionally separated. "All it would have taken was for one of us to say two words, 'I'm leaving.' But in your prayer seminar you said we needed to ask forgiveness from those we hurt and forgive those who have hurt us." She went on to say that she and her husband turned to each other, asked forgiveness of one another, and then forgave each other. "At that instant the Lord healed our marriage. We had come to the seminar as two independent married people and left as one in mind and heart. Praise God. We have two sons who would have been devastated by divorce."

Someone once told me, "A good marriage is made up not of two good lovers—but of two good forgivers!"

But family rifts and bad marriages are not always mended by forgiveness and love. My heart broke as we were asked to pray for a thirty-five-year-old Christian woman who was bringing up alone the baby she had as an unwed young teenager. Ostracized by family and friends, she was almost breaking emotionally under the strain. Even her mother had refused to speak to her since it happened.

When They Won't Be Reconciled

No matter how hard we try, there are those who refuse to be reconciled to us—the marriage partner who files for divorce and marries another, the parent who never again accepts the disowned child, the runaway child who severs all ties, the family member who refuses to break the angry silence of many years.

What do we do now? Romans 12:18 spells out our responsibility in these situations. "If possible, *so far as it depends on you*, be at peace with all men" (NASB, emphasis mine). In other words, we must do absolutely everything possible to bring about reconciliation with that person. But in real life, this is not always possible. However, whether others will or will not be at peace with us, God says we must be at peace with them.

A promising young seminary graduate just starting to serve his first church was devastated when his bride left him for her career, and she now admits to being deeply in love with another man. His dreams, his hopes, and, he is afraid, his career are lying shattered at his feet. In agony of soul, he has searched for reasons—and solutions. He has exhausted every avenue of wooing and begging, only to be repulsed time and time again.

What then? There comes a time when there is nothing left but prayer—two kinds. First, a *prayer of relinquishment.* Just before I spoke at a church luncheon, I couldn't understand why so many were weeping as a lovely, articulate woman gave a short devotional on Catherine Marshall's "Prayer of Relinquishment." But the wife of the pastor of this beautiful church whispered the reason: "She was the wife of the former pastor, who ran away with his secretary and has just married her." Yes, when the one God joined in one flesh with you is married to another, it is time for the prayer of relinquishment.

A pastor at the National Prayer Assembly of India wept openly as he shared with us how he, just that day, had forgiven a member of his church who had twice put a knife to his throat to kill him. Then he wrote to me: "That rich man has closed the doors of my preaching there . . . but I prayed with broken heart in tears, 'Oh, Lord, forgive that man's mistakes

and sins. Help me, Lord, to accept him as my own brother.' "
Then he told me how he went to him and said, "Please, my
dear brother, forgive me; I love you very much and I pray
for you." But the offender just said, "You do not come to
my house. Go away from here."

But this pastor in India also discovered the other kind of
prayer to use when all seems hopeless—intercessory prayer
for them. Jesus said, "Pray for them which despitefully use
you" (Matt. 5:44).

I am continuously amazed at the flood of phone calls I receive from Christian wives whose husbands have found other
women. Over and over, they tell me how they had remained
faithful and prayed for years for their unfaithful mates; and
even now, they are continuing to pray for them—no matter
how despitefully they have been used. And the calls and letters
from those who have been despitefully used at work, at school,
in their neighborhood, even in Christian organizations—still
praying *for* those who have wronged them—astounds me.
They are following Jesus' admonition to pray for those who
despitefully use them!

Amazing Results of Oneness

Jesus knew why He demanded reconciliation and oneness.
He knew the fantastic results of being reconciled to each other.
In His high-priestly prayer recorded in John 17, He gave us
His reasons for praying that we might be one (John 17:20–
23). Jesus knew that so many of the things we need and hope
for are the results of being reconciled. They are *that* in our
oneness we can have the same relationship as the Father and
Son have. *That* we can have the privileged position of actually
being *in* that Father-Son relationship of oneness. Our unity
will prove *that* God sent Jesus. And Jesus gave us the glory
God gave Him that we may also be one. *That* we may be
perfected in unity so *that* the world will know God sent Jesus,
and *that* He loves the world just as He loves His Son, Jesus.
For what more could we ask?

But even more amazingly, the credibility of Jesus in the
world hangs on our unity! So, when we are tempted to pray,
"God, with whom should I be reconciled?" He will unhesitat-
ingly answer, "Everybody!"

Closing Prayer

Father, I'm sorry for living as if my broken relationships with people did not matter to You. Please forgive me. Help me to make reconciliation as far as it is possible for me to do. I promise to pray for those who have despitefully used me. Thank You that Jesus insisted on the reconciliation of members of His body, not so that we could become one, but because *we are one. And I promise to seek out the real body of Your Son, Jesus, and practice the oneness He died to give us.*

In Jesus' name, **Amen.**

9

WHEN GOD ANSWERS . . .

Make Restitution

Although God no longer holds us accountable to Himself for the sins He has forgiven, we still are responsible to the human beings we have hurt.

After praying, "God, I have sinned," and taking the steps of repenting and being reconciled to Him and others, are we absolved of all further responsibility and action? No. We still have a responsibility to the one against whom we have sinned.

This is the step of restitution. It is making amends, making good for a loss or damage. It is giving back to the rightful owner something that has been taken away. When we have sinned, it is our duty to make amends to the one victimized by our sinning.

While we must be reconciled to God when we sin, restitution is only made to the persons against whom we have sinned. There is no way we can repay God for violating His holiness. All we can do is repent because we have hurt Him so deeply and love Him so much that we will do everything in our power to restore our relationship with Him. Then we can serve Him with a new passion, making up for the lost days or opportunities. But our human relationships are different.

Reconciliation to people against whom we have sinned or committed a crime usually includes making restitution of some kind.

Thinking of Our Victim

As we study and teach the biblical accounts of David's sin, we tend to ignore Bathsheba's side. But David did not; he finally got around to thinking about her.

When the Lord sent Nathan to David to rebuke him for his sin with Bathsheba and for having her husband killed, Nathan told David a story. It concerned a rich man who killed the only lamb of a poor neighbor to feed his guests instead of one from his own large flock. David burned with anger and cried, "As the LORD lives, surely the man who has done this deserves to die. And he must *make restitution* for the lamb fourfold, because he did this thing and had no compassion" (2 Sam. 12:5–6, NASB). Then, as Nathan said, "You are the man!" David was devastated and repented of his horrendous sins.

But the results of his sin extended to his victim, Bathsheba. When David recognized himself as the sinner and repented, Nathan said, "The LORD also has taken away your sin; you shall not die. However, because by this deed you have given occasion to the enemies of the LORD to blaspheme, the child also that is born to you shall surely die" (2 Sam. 12:13–14, NASB). So, although God did forgive David's sins, because of his sin, the innocent victim, Bathsheba, lost in death the two humans closest to her—her husband and her child.

David finally realized that repenting before God was not the end of his responsibility. As king, he had said that the rich man who had killed the poor man's lamb had to make restitution. And now he realized that he, being the man Nathan was talking about, also had to make restitution. So he turned to the one he had hurt—Bathsheba. Second Samuel 12:24 tells us that after the child died, "Then David comforted his wife Bathsheba" (NASB).

There was a point after the child's death that David stopped having a "pity party." He stopped looking only at what had happened to himself—because he got caught. David saw that his lust for Bathsheba had twice caused deep sorrow in her. When he had her husband killed on the front lines,

Bathsheba was in deep anguish and mourning, like any other bereaved widow. David's sin not only caused her to be widowed, but it also caused the death of her child conceived in his sin.

The Victim's Hurt

My phone rings many, many times with calls from the devastated victims of sinning children, mates, or others begging for prayer support. I wait silently as the grief so wells up within the caller that words are unutterable. Or I listen with my heart aching as they sob uncontrollably, trying to ask for prayer. Their lives have been shattered; and, while I understand that no child or parent or mate is perfect, there usually seems to be one who is grievously sinning and causing the heartache. There *are* innocent people being hurt.

I held a grieving mother in my arms after a seminar as she related how her seemingly fine Christian daughter had turned her back on God and was trying every conceivable thrill of the world on the streets of one of our large cities. Then I felt this mother's whole body shudder violently at the repulsive mental picture of all that filthy sin in her darling child. She was a teenager fulfilling her own evil desires but was completely oblivious, or at least insensitive, to what she was doing to her parents.

I remember the chagrined agony of a mother as I sat in the local police station with her and her ninth-grade son as he was given jobs in the community to make restitution for stealing "just little things" from his employer. "Where have I gone wrong?" she moaned. "Where did I fail? I have tried so hard to live and teach biblical values in our home." Here was a parent giving her very lifeblood to her child—only to have him repay with a lifestyle producing anguish and even guilt in her.

The sinning son or daughter must see the devastating hurt they are causing their heartbroken parents. The untrustworthy employee must face the ruptured trust of the employer's faith; the sinning spouse must admit the pain of broken marriage vows; the sinning pastor must see the hurt to his congregation. The sinning parent must be aware of the deep hurts he or she is causing in the children, and the criminal the loss of possessions, dignity, or life he has inflicted upon his victim.

For more than a year, I have prayed on the phone with Kaye, whose husband fell in love with another woman in their church. And, while Kaye watched from her seat in the choir loft, the situation progressed from that of girlfriend to a lover, then to the divorce, and now with the new wife all but snuggling with Kaye's former husband during church services. The pastor had watched it all from his vantage point in the pulpit and later performed the marriage ceremony with his blessing—evidently without questioning whether it was God's will that the already-married couple stay married. And evidently, the pastor did so without remembering Jesus' teaching in Matthew 19:6, where He said, "What therefore God has joined together, let no man separate" (NASB), and the words in Malachi 2:16, " 'For I hate divorce,' says the LORD" (NASB).

Those agonizing months of seeing the romance progress were times of deep self-examination for Kaye—as with most with whom I pray. She constantly kept asking me what she had done wrong, where she had failed, how could she improve so as to mend the rift. One of the most difficult things to deal with in these phone calls is the victims' search for answers from God on how to change themselves, when the sinning mates seem oblivious to any problem in themselves.

The women I talk with not only are working to become better mates, but they are struggling to keep the children together and care for their physical and emotional needs. Then in addition to all this, they are pouring out their hearts in prayer for their wayward partners.

My own saintly mother told me her feelings when my father confessed to her his unfaithfulness. "I always had said that my husband would never do anything like that. I believed he could do nothing wrong. I had complete trust in him, my bridegroom," she wept. "The thing that hurt the most was lost trust. Being betrayed by the one I had absolute, complete faith in. My bridegroom! I wanted to die—to jump off a bridge—to kill myself."

Welling up within me as she talked were God's words in Malachi 2:15, where He almost thunders, "Let no one deal treacherously against the wife of your youth" (NASB). Marriage vows are shattered, bodily purity is desecrated, and lifetime promises are broken for the mate still believing in the sanctity of marriage as one of life's most valuable possessions!

Frequently, the victim remains skeptical, unable ever to trust again. But not so with my Christlike mother. Although my father was not a Christian, I watched in amazement as she forgave him and little by little restored him and their marriage with her astonishingly selfless love.

What Do You Expect?

Prisoners often expect to be pardoned or paroled early after being sentenced regardless of the injury to their victims. But a pastor speaking at a recent National Religious Broadcasters convention made an important point when he said, "The criminal should stay in prison as long as the victim has to stay in the hospital."

A story I am told so frequently is that a husband leaves home, lives with another woman for a while, then comes back and acts as if nothing had happened. He feels as if he has a perfect right to expect all the comforts of home—just the way it was before. One woman told me that her husband comes and goes like this and becomes absolutely incensed if she so much as suggests that it may not be right and is hurting her.

Jesus told of a much more realistic expectation by the prodigal son who, after squandering his estate from his father in riotous living in a far country, came to his senses and went back home—*expecting* to be made just a hired hand. Even though his father embraced him and kissed him, the son cried, "Father, I have sinned against heaven and in your sight; I am no longer worthy to be called your son" (Luke 15:21, NASB).

We, too, should not *expect* to be welcomed back with open arms when we have caused grief and anxiety in someone. We should understand that the human response from our victim is more apt to be like that of the prodigal's elder brother who was angry and unwilling for a restored relationship. We should be extremely grateful when the victim is willing to forgive, accept us back, and restore our relationship.

Accept Responsibility

When I teach the biblical responsibility of the one sinned against to forgive (*What Happens When Women Pray*) and what the serious consequences are to us if we don't forgive (*Gaining through Losing*), people say to me, "But what about *them?*" Well, this chapter is about "them"—the responsibility of the sinner who has caused the hurt.

Basically, it is the selfishness of the one sinning that causes the hurt the victim must endure. The current popular philosophy even among some Christians is to think only of being fulfilled themselves, doing what feels good, with little or no concern for those they may be hurting. It is the philosophy of humanism which is rampant or so-called Christian humanism, by which these Christians are living diametrically opposed to God's biblical rules.

I recall the depth of our prayers for a pregnant wife who was on the verge of collapsing emotionally because her husband was having an affair. The girlfriend decided to have a baby shower for the coming baby—but didn't invite the mother-to-be! Then, when all the guests had left, she and the husband lay down in the midst of the baby gifts and had sex. The strain of the pregnancy plus this unbelievably inhuman treatment made many fear for the wife's health as she was almost breaking emotionally. This was fatherhood—without the least concern or responsibility for the emotional harm he was causing to his wife and unborn child!

Sinners must see themselves as the wrongdoers. They must accept the fact that they are guilty of having hurt another person or perhaps many others. The one who has caused the emotional, mental, and perhaps physical suffering must accept responsibility for the one he or she has devastated—realizing that this person needs to be healed and that restitution is imperative.

Have you sinned by stealing someone else's reputation by passing on false or only partially true rumors about them? Have you undermined a minister God has called because of your vicious criticism of him? Have you destroyed somebody else's self-worth because this was the only way you could feed and satisfy your own pride and ego? Have you gotten ahead and succeeded by trampling a co-worker? Is your sin with someone of the opposite sex, in thought or deed, devastating your mate? Is your child's emotional well-being shattered because you are selfishly living in sin? Are you causing anguish and undeserved guilt in your parents because of your lifestyle? Is stepping on somebody else the only way you can get what you want and what fulfills you? Then restitution to that person is in order.

Make Restitution

In colonial America, Jonathan Edwards considered restitution an ongoing obligation and failure to make it an ongoing sin. He said, "I exhort those who are conscious in themselves that they have wronged their neighbor to make restitution. This is a duty the obligation to which is exceedingly plain. . . . A man who hath gotten anything from another wrongfully, goes on to wrong him every day that he neglects to restore it, when he has opportunity to do it." [1]

After acknowledging responsibility for our victim's hurts, it is time to take active steps to make amends. And there are those sinners and criminals who have accepted this responsibility and have courageously acted upon it, making restitution.

Prison Fellowship is sponsoring successful Community Service Projects in which Christian prisoners are released into communities for a couple of weeks to repair homes of needy citizens and to participate in other helpful projects—to make restitution.

The Reverend Sam Hines, a powerful pastor in Washington, D.C., whose church already provides foster care for homeless children and breakfast five days a week for hundreds of the neighborhood's homeless, hosted a Prison Fellowship Community Service Project. Five Christian inmates spent two weeks repairing the home of a needy, nine-member family on the block. The response from the community was overwhelming, and even the mayor of the District of Columbia, Marion Barry, commended Prison Fellowship's community service.

When the project was over, Pastor Hines said, "People see convicts negatively—but this project exploded that myth." People had seen prisoners—changed by the living Christ—bringing practical demonstrations of love in the form of hammers and nails and fresh, clean paint to a grimy home in need.

---

1. Henry Rogers, ed., *The Works of Jonathan Edwards,* Vol. 2, rev. Edward Hickman (London: Ball, Arnold, and Co., 1840), p. 226.

But most important, it gave the prisoners themselves the privilege of making restitution, of making amends for some of the hurt they had caused the community. Not because they had to—but because they wanted to. They also gained a positive self-image about themselves. Restitution!

Daniel Van Ness, president of Justice Fellowship in Washington, D.C., informed me that, at this writing, there is a bill being drafted by one of our United States congressmen that "would have federal minimum security prisoners leave their confinement during the day to work. Of course," he wrote, "they would be well-supervised. The money they receive would be divided between the victim, the prisoner's family, the government (to pay room and board), and some savings for the prisoner. The benefits to the victim and community are obvious," he continued. "Victims would be paid back, and the community would have its costs reduced. But I think there is also a great benefit to the offender, not the least of which is the opportunity to make right the wrong."

How marvelous it would be to finally have a restitution program and one that would benefit the victim, the prisoner's family, the government, and the criminal!

John Calvin said, "In whatever way, therefore, a man should have committed an offense, whereby another is made poorer, he is commanded to make good the loss." [2]

Mary Kay Beard is one who has made good many losses and is now giving her whole life to prisoners. At Charles Colson's Prison Fellowship staff retreat, I spent many hours with Mary Kay, a successful and effective state director of this organization. "My whole life is restitution now," Mary Kay said to me.

But she has not always been bringing Christ into prisons and working with inmates, their families, and released prisoners. Mary Kay is an ex-con herself who was sentenced to serve twenty-one years in prison for armed robbery of mainly cash and diamonds. She was wanted in five states and by the federal government, and there was a contract on her life from the underworld.

She was abused as a child by her alcoholic father who had broken her back, every one of her ribs, and her nose twice.

---

2. John Calvin, *Commentary on the Four Last Books of Moses*, vol. 5 (Grand Rapids, Mich.: Wm. B. Eerdmans Publishing Co., n.d.), p. 149.

Running away from home at fifteen, then marrying the man she later discovered was a gambler and a thief, Mary Kay traveled for five years with him in a continuous crime spree. Beautiful clothes, furs, jewels, and custom-built cars fulfilled all her girlhood dreams. Then the man she worshiped left her and was soon arrested. Eight months later she, too, was in jail.

Mary Kay, however, was transformed in prison when one day she slipped from her metal bunk onto her knees on the concrete floor of her cell and gave her life to Jesus. She wrote, "As tears streamed unchecked down my face, a flood of joy filled my whole being. I felt light, as though I'd been loosed from a mighty anchor. At that moment on March 16, 1973, God set me free—free from a terrible weight of guilt and shame, and free from the enslavement of sin!"

Graduating with honors in the first group of inmates to participate in the prison-college program at Julia Tutwiler Prison for women, she has gone on to become the first woman in the United States to receive a graduate degree while serving time in a prison.

More Than Legalistic Responsibility

Mary Kay now devotes her life to those still in concrete and spiritual prisons. And the exuberance and joy with which she bounces and beams made me know it was not just legalistic responsibility—but wanting to—that motivates her.

"Angel Tree," one of Prison Fellowship's most successful programs, was originated by Mary Kay. Since prison inmates rarely can buy any Christmas presents for their children, these children are asked to write down the four things they want most for Christmas. The requests are then recorded on paper angels that are hung on Christmas trees placed in churches, shopping malls, or other public places by Prison Fellowship volunteers. Then people, taking an angel from the tree, purchase one or more of these gifts, which are wrapped and delivered to the children by Prison Fellowship staff and volunteers.

It is incredible what this now nationwide project is accomplishing. Children who feel forsaken suddenly are remembered, ever-widening rifts between incarcerated parents and their children are narrowed, and many desperate needs are filled. During Christmas 1985, Angel Trees provided Christmas presents for 31,500 children of inmates. The response of these children when the gifts were delivered was absolutely overwhelming.

I asked Mary what the children requested and she replied, "It's amazing. Sometimes it's just a pencil box for school the parent can't supply. One adolescent asked for a *new* item of underclothing, which she had never owned in her whole life. Another young girl asked for just one thing—to be able to visit her daddy in prison in another state for Christmas. Most people puzzled over that 'angel' request and passed it by. But an eighth-grade Sunday school class picked it off the tree, worked to raise the money, and sent her to see her daddy for Christmas!"

I asked Mary whether this project was in any manner her way of making restitution. Surprised at this possible motivation, she said she needed some time to think it through. When we met the next day, she had the answer: "There's no question about it. Yes, this is my way of helping the whole prison population." Then Mary reflected sadly, "Christmas is the hardest time of the year to be away from children and to be absolutely unable to bring any happiness into their lives. It was especially hard to watch mothers in prison receive perhaps a little gift of toothpaste from a caring church group or individual, and then give it to their child for Christmas— the only gift they had."

This is far more than legalistic responsibility. To me, Mary Kay seemed to be a tremendous example of the apostle John's admonition in 1 John 3:18 to live out Jesus' love, "Little children, let us not love with word or with tongue, but in *deed* and truth" (NASB).

Mary Kay also had a lot of restitution to make to her own family. She explained to me, "I had created division between my sisters while I was living with them by lying about what each had said in certain situations."

And she told me that when she prayed, "Lord, where did I go wrong?" He answered by telling her to write a letter, making restitution to her two older sisters. She wrote and rewrote letter after letter, always including in each one something that justified her actions. But God would always tell her that it was not right. "It was when I finally could write confessing it all as a total lie that the Holy Spirit let me put it in the mail." Although it was more than four years before one sister responded, accepting her apology, Mary Kay had obeyed God's answer to her prayer—to make restitution.

It was two years after the crime had been committed that God brought to Mary Kay's mind her need to make restitution for having misused a telephone credit card for more than one hundred dollars. But she had to ask God to bring to her mind the exact date and the phone number she needed to know in order to make restitution. His answer was to have her mother check all her old phone bills, which, surprisingly, included the phone number to which Mary Kay had charged all those bills. Mary Kay was making twenty-five dollars a month in her prison work-release job, and it took exactly four months to make that restitution. But make it she did!

Restitution is not just paying fines, sending alimony checks, serving a prison sentence, or begrudgingly paying back what we have stolen. It springs from desire of the heart. Restitution is not made from duty—but from love.

Not Always Easy

"To make restitution may open yourself to more liability than you think you can deal with," Mary Kay told me. "When I was wanted in four states but had not yet come to trial, I knew that if I confessed to one crime it would have shown that I had been in Raleigh, North Carolina, and would have implicated me in several other crimes. But I finally could write to that sheriff and admit that I had stolen that car there, so the items could be returned to their rightful owner." But she told me that although she was willing to pay the additional price, God graciously protected her from further charges of more crimes in that area at the time. Restitution may not be easy!

One restitution experience was particularly difficult for her because of the *victim's partial guilt*. After becoming a Christian, Mary Kay pleaded guilty to the crime of stealing cash and jewelry from a member of a certain town's "First Church." But her victim accused Mary Kay of stealing a ring that the woman had had in her safety deposit vault all along, collecting the insurance for the supposed theft. Mary Kay had asked this woman's forgiveness for breaking into her home, frightening her, and stealing not only her possessions but her security in her home as well. But her victim refused to forgive Mary Kay, claiming the worst part was having lost the ring—which, of course, she had all along.

More than a year later, the warden allowed Mary Kay to speak to a Christian Women's Club in that city, and this woman had been invited to attend. With reporters and the chief of detention watching, Mary Kay shared her testimony. The victim's neighbor then asked Mary Kay if she wasn't going to ask for forgiveness since the woman claimed that her life started to fall apart at the time of the robbery and, although her husband forgave Mary Kay before he died, the woman was now a desperately bitter widow.

Mary Kay knew that she had been denied forgiveness and swallowed hard to keep from revealing the truth and incriminating her victim. In this case, it was time for the *victim* to make restitution by asking Mary to forgive her and returning the insurance money. Mary's responsibility ended when she had asked for forgiveness and was paying back what she actually stole. The victim's problems were her own because of her guilt in the crime and her unforgiveness.

Mary Kay's husband, Don, an ex-con who had served two terms for embezzlement and business-related crimes, joined us at that Prison Fellowship retreat. Together, they explained their *joint restitution program.*

First, they prayed asking God how they should go about making restitution. He answered with a specific plan which they immediately put into practice. The first 10 percent of their budget would go to God, then they agreed that 60 percent would be sufficient for their household budget, and that the other 30 percent would go to those from whom they had stolen.

Then they carefully sought out and contacted their victims, initially taking care of those who were personally harmed and who suffered personal loss, dividing the 30 percent among them little by little, month by month. Restitution is not paying a fine that goes to the treasury of the community but repaying the victim.

Jesus Makes a Difference

Mary Kay and Don reminded me of Zacchaeus, the rich tax-gatherer who climbed a tree that he might see Jesus. Zacchaeus and other tax collectors did not receive a salary for their work, but they collected as much money as they could so that they would have a handsome rake-off after paying the Roman government its appointed sum. But when Zacchaeus had "received Jesus gladly," he made this startling declaration of his restitution intentions to Jesus, "Behold, Lord, half of my possessions I will give to the poor, and if I have defrauded anyone of anything, I will give back four times as much" (Luke 19:8, NASB).

Surprisingly, there is no indication of Jesus demanding that Zacchaeus make restitution. It was simply that once he came into a right relationship with his Lord, all the cheating of his past life loomed before him; and his first thought was to make amends to those he had hurt.

Evidently, he did not think only of clearing his own conscience by making restitution, but a new love and compassion for his victims sprang up within him. In place of greed, Zacchaeus seemed to discover the thrill of seeing his victims repaid, and perhaps even lifted out of their poverty.

Should we today do less than Zacchaeus? Should we not only have the blush of a first love that comes with new life in Jesus, but also an ever-growing awareness of how we damage, hurt, and wound our victims even in everyday life?

Since Zacchaeus's words, "I give" and "I give back," are both in the present tense in the Greek, we know that he intended a future ongoing process of making restitution. Should we not also strive to keep alive that sensitivity to those hurts we bring to people—even those we love?

For the Sinner's Benefit

As I talked with Don Beard at the Prison Fellowship staff retreat, I was impressed by his insight into the importance to the criminal himself of making restitution. "I am at the point now in my restitution that I can walk around without fear of whom I might run into," he said, smiling victoriously.

"Did all those to whom you made restitution respond in the same way?" I asked Don.

"Oh, no. When I went to them and said that I had a responsibility for the past but could only repay a little at a time, their responses varied. One man was offended. Another former business acquaintance whom I had cheated greatly was overwhelmed. He said that he knew from my actions I was sincere and forgave me the whole debt. Amazingly," Don continued, "those people I harmed the most forgave the most!"

Then Don agreed with me that the victim's response has nothing to do with the responsibility to make restitution. The responsibility is the offender's—but also the rewards are his.

"Making restitution is very rewarding to myself," said Don. *"It has validated what I did in private with God as I repented."* He explained further, "Restitution gives substance to your repentance." Then, seemingly reflecting on this whole process, he said softly, "Repentance without restitution is pretty hollow."

Don knew about repentance. He had repented when he accepted Christ as his Savior while a prisoner. And then as a Christian, he had repented deeply over the hurts he had caused in so many people. And he had learned well that complete restoration never can come to the offender until there has been the lifting of the guilt in one's own eyes by making restitution.

Then Mary Kay and Don chimed in together, "Restitution is for the criminal's benefit. It is healing and cleansing!"

Is there restitution you have to make?

Closing Prayer

Oh, God, forgive me for being insensitive to those I have hurt. Forgive my selfishness. Father, bring to my mind all those to whom I need to make restitution. God, I will wait in silence for You to bring to my mind the steps You want me to take. Please give me Jesus' love for them and Your courage to be obedient to Your expectations of me.

In Jesus' name, **Amen.**

10

Restore That Sinner

When catching a sister or brother sinning, how often we pray, "Oh, God, what do I do now?" And the surprising answer from God is already recorded in the Bible. "Restore that sinner!"

> Brethren, even if a man is caught in any trespass, you who are spiritual, restore such a one in a spirit of gentleness (Gal. 6:1, NASB).

What does it mean to restore? Paul had in mind here the mending of something that had been damaged. Restoration is the responsibility of those Christians surrounding the sinner. Repentance, reconciliation, and restitution are all the responsibility of the sinner; but, shockingly, restoration very likely must be done by the one sinned against, and it may even be the victim's job.

However, restoration does not begin while the person is sinning. It is when he or she is "caught" trespassing that the process begins. There can be no real restoration without the sinner fulfilling the other three "R's" preceding it—repentance, reconciliation, and restitution. Paul leaves no excuse in his teaching for Christians who are sinning, but makes it clear that the person who has sinned can be restored. But it is only the sinner whom God has accepted back through His forgiveness that we should accept back and restore.

This seems to be a lost teaching in recent years. We have been handling the sinning brother or sister one of two ways. Either we have ignored the sin, finding it much more comfortable not to become involved, or we have followed the scriptural injunction to rebuke him but with no further concern for the repentant one's well-being and restoration.

Although sin is not to be tolerated, there are definite steps the Christian church must take when a brother or sister sins. And the final step in this whole process is restoring the sinner to fellowship and ministry.

Jesus told His followers in Luke 17:3, "Be on your guard! If your brother sins, rebuke him; and *if he repents,* forgive him" (NASB). It is when the sinner repents that Christian action begins.

Who Restores That Sinner?

At a "Lord, Change Me" seminar a few years ago, during a Bible reading exercise, God stopped me at Galatians 6:1, "Restore such a one in a spirit of gentleness" (NASB). As I prayed asking Him who it was He wanted me to restore, His immediate answer was the name of a close friend. Whenever the Lord gives a command as clear as this to me, I immediately promise Him I'll do it—which I did that day.

Then I asked God what needed to be restored, and His answer flooding through my mind was, "Vigor, leadership, self-esteem, shoulders back, and a posture of confidence again." So, for more than two years, I have been actively involved in restoring my friend. And although the price has been high, the rewards and joys for me are indescribable as I've watched one by one those qualities being abundantly restored to my friend.

God, through Paul, gave the "spiritual" Christians in the churches in Galatia the job of restoring sinners. I remember recoiling at that word *spiritual.* In all honesty, I could not see myself as "spiritual." Although I knew God divided Christians into these categories, it felt like horrible pride for me to do so. But it is true that while no Christian is perfect, there are some who are striving to be Christlike while others are living in defiance of His laws. It is to these "spiritual" Christians that God gives the restoring role.

Also, in the great forgiving formula in 2 Corinthians 2:5–11, it is the grieved Christian who is to comfort, get underneath, and buoy up the one who has done the grieving. And it is the Christian whom a brother has something against who is to go to that brother before bringing his offering to God.

Now, if we are not willing to obey God and restore the sinner, then we obviously don't qualify as being spiritual in His eyes. We may prefer to remain bitter, especially if we are the one sinned against. Then we are breaking God's command in Ephesians 4:31 to "let all bitterness and wrath and anger . . . be put away from you, along with all malice" (NASB). Which, of course, marks us as unspiritual also. And a Christian living in sin hardly is in a position or eligible to restore a sinning brother or sister.

"I Don't Want To"

There also is the possibility that we don't want the sinner restored. We may prefer to say, "Good, you got what was coming to you. Squirm in the results of your sin! Retaliation is what you will get from me, not restoration!" But restoration, not retaliation or retribution, is God's New Testament command to us. "See that no one repays another with evil for evil, but always seek after that which is good for one another and for all men" (1 Thess. 5:15, NASB). Then again in Romans 12:17, "Never pay back evil for evil to anyone" (NASB).

There are many reasons why we knowingly or subconsciously really do not want the sinner to be restored. As long as they are not restored, we appear so much more spiritual in contrast to them. We, the victims, get so much more sympathy for the burden we are carrying if they remain in their sinning state. And people may even compliment us on what a great job we are doing holding them up.

Or, perhaps we need the sinner to keep depending on us. We need to be the strong, victorious, forgiving leader. It helps our own self-image when they are groveling at our feet in remorse, shame, and defeat.

I was surprised at the warning to me included in Galatians 6:1, "Looking to yourself, *lest* you too be tempted" (NASB). Reading verse 3, I cried, "Oh, God, forgive me for thinking I'm better than the one I'm restoring. Search my heart lest I be tempted, too—before I am."

Then, of course, there is the possibility of our being jealous of the repentant sinner being restored to a great ministry, feeling they have no right to achieve once more and perhaps even surpass us. But, no matter what our excuses, God says in His word, *"Restore that sinner!"*

Who Needs Restoring?

We must be careful to identify the sinner about whom Paul is writing in Galatians 6:1. Restoration is possible only in the life of a Christian. Being restored to an upright state (2 Tim. 3:16) is not possible for one still in the state of sin into which he or she was born. What non-Christians need is regeneration—when all sin is forgiven as they repent and accept Christ. Then they are accepted into the body of Christ for nurturing.

Paul was careful to tell us in 1 Corinthians 5:12–13 not to judge the outsider, because God would. Jesus also said in John 3:18 that the one not believing on Him is condemned already. The restoration process is not for him. We are to win that one to Jesus—who at the moment is making that person a new creation in Himself.

My non-Christian father sinned against my mother for many years; and even though she forgave him—and there was complete reconciliation in their marriage, and although he did his best to make restitution for what he had done to her—my father could not be restored to an upright state. It was only after he asked God to forgive all his sins and asked Jesus to become his Savior and Lord (Mark 1:15) that we as a family could watch his restoration begin.

How Do Humans Restore Sinners?

Now that we know restoring the sinning brother or sister is not optional, we ask God, "But how do we go about restoring such a one?" The Bible is full of God's instructions on this oft-neglected subject.

Rebuking the sinner is His first instruction. Just as the Lord sent Nathan to rebuke David after he had sinned, so God also sends people today. Sometimes He sends a Nathan into our lives, and other times He calls on us to be the Nathan.

When Nathan told David he had not just sinned against Uriah but had despised the word of the Lord by doing evil in His sight, David cried out, "I have sinned against the Lord" (2 Sam. 12:13, NASB). And David, accepting Nathan's rebuke, had taken the first step toward restoration.

How important it is to listen to those whom God sends to us. Jesus in Luke 16:19–31 told His followers the story of a rich man calling from his place of torment after death, begging Abraham to send Lazarus to warn his brothers to repent. But Abraham answered, "If they do not listen to Moses and the Prophets, neither will they be persuaded if someone rises from the dead" (Luke 16:31, NASB).

Paul, giving instructions as to what to do with an erring brother or sister, concludes with, "And yet, do not regard him as an enemy, but admonish him as a brother" (2 Thess. 3:15, NASB).

Jesus tells His followers in Luke 17:3, "Be on your guard! If your brother sins, rebuke him" (NASB). So the first step in people restoring a sinning brother or sister is to admonish and warn.

Restore by forgiving. Rebuking the sinning brother is not all we are to do to restore him. Jesus follows this admonition to rebuke the sinning brother with the words, "And if he repents, forgive him" (Luke 17:3, NASB).

The restoration process demands that the one doing the restoring forgive the one being restored. Without genuine forgiveness, the whole process will be a sham; and the insincerity of the restorer will be sensed by the one hopefully being restored.

The step of forgiveness in restoring the sinner may be the most difficult one to take. Sometimes, we resent the person being restored, having deep unresolved feelings that he, or she, "doesn't deserve to be forgiven and restored after that awful sin." But we cannot begin to restore a repentant sinner until we have forgiven him or her.

I watched the hurt in a close friend as his wife was having

an affair with a mutual family friend, finally leaving him and their children. Then came the reconciliation period when the husband took her back into their home. One day, the husband and I happened to meet. With his face flushed with deep emotion and his eyes wet with tears, he smiled through it all as he showed me a Bible passage. "Look what the Lord gave me! See, it tells me how I'm to forgive her. And, Mrs. Chris, I did! I did! I've forgiven her!" How exciting now, a couple of years later, to see this marriage and the erring wife completely and joyously restored!

For me, the hardest part of obeying while working with the person God gave me to restore came one afternoon when that person just exploded in confession to me that I was the one against whom that friend had sinned. Although I actually had known about it for years, there always had been that one's denial of the situation. Although I truly had forgiven when it happened, suddenly hearing the awful details sent me reeling in shock. And only God enabled me to stand unflinchingly on all the previous forgivenesses; never once did I feel a twinge of unforgiveness that day.

In the last ten years during our prayer seminar teaching on forgiving, I have seen literally hundreds of marriages restored and snatched from divorce proceedings by the act of forgiving an erring spouse.

Restoration to usefulness in God's kingdom is possible only after involved Christians forgive the repentant leader or layperson. I missed a convention speech as I sat listening to a beautiful Christian leader tell me of the bitter circumstance she had just left at home. Her fourteen-year-old daughter was soon to give birth to a baby fathered by their church's youth director—who was married and had a child of his own. He had come to their home to counsel their daughter, had taken her into the bedroom, and she came out pregnant.

Devastated, he deeply repented before God, appeared before the church body asking for their forgiveness, and unremittingly did all he could to make it right with the family and the girl against whom he had sinned.

This mother recounted that just before she left for this convention he had come to see how her little girl was doing. Then she repeated to me the incredible thing she said to him: "You have a theological education and were called by God to serve Him the rest of your life. Now, when Satan gets other people to say that you have forfeited the right to serve God because of the awful thing you did, you look them right in the eye and say, 'Oh, but even her mother forgave me!' "

A highly qualified administrator had been hired by a Christian college, only to be fired at the insistence of its ruling board because of a past immoral act. Although he had deeply repented to God, to his wife, and before his church publicly and had been forgiven and taken back by all, the members of the college board still were skeptical and understandably protective of the reputation of their school and the possible influence on the student body. But even though he definitely had turned from his former lifestyle, he was not given the opportunity to be restored to ministry.

After sinning, how many Christians, gifted by God for His kingdom's work, are using those talents in the world because Christians refused to do their part in obeying God's command to forgive and restore after the offender had taken the steps of repentance, reconciliation, and restitution?

Restore by what we are. It is not only what we say but what we are in our relationship to God that is extremely important in our human restoration of repentant sinners. The ones being restored will "catch" what we are, much more than what we tell them. Our unshakable trust and faith in God; our striving to be holy in spite of all the ugly circumstances in which we are living or people with whom we are associating; an upbeat, victorious attitude toward life; a sweet spirit of gentleness permeating our whole being—these will help restore that sinner.

I watched this in my mother, one of the greatest restorers God ever put on earth. Unshakable, childlike trust in God no matter how her world was falling apart; never wavering in her faith as she restored sinning relatives and my repentant father; tenderly caring for him in his last, bedridden years—my mother!

In fact, it was during a period when I was deeply seeking God's holiness for myself and praying for revival, that the one I was restoring said, "It was watching your striving to be holy, and my realization that I am not spiritually eligible to be part of revival, that I couldn't stand. It led to my being unable to stand my deceit—and ultimately to confess."

*Restore by praying **for** that sinner.* Praying is the most powerful thing we can do to restore the sinner. Why? Because it releases the God of the universe to reach down and touch that repentant sinner with His omnipotent restoration.

Also, there may be times in the depth of guilt and remorse that the sinner is spiritually or emotionally unable to pray for himself or herself; and then our prayers will be all the prayer there is. There also may be times that praying is the only thing we can do.

However, this is praying *for,* not *about,* the repentant sinner. Jesus exhorted His followers in Matthew 5:44 to "Pray *for* them which despitefully use you." It is rather easy to pray *about* the person we are restoring, but sincere intercession *for* them requires much more of us. We can experience a deep agony of soul as we wrestle in prayer for them. By interceding *for* the sinning Christian, we enter into the very work Christ Himself is now engaged in at the right hand of the Father.

After witnessing much sinning by God's chosen people, the prophet Samuel said to them, "God forbid that *I* should sin against the Lord by ceasing to pray for you (1 Sam. 12:23, NASB). This also is true of the "spiritual" Christians God calls to restore sinning brothers and sisters.

Aradam Tedla, whose escape from Ethiopia was written up in the December 1983 issue of *Reader's Digest* magazine, smiled at me following my "Gaining through Losing" seminar in Washington, D.C. After most of his friends were executed or imprisoned without the right to defend themselves, and after his own release from prison, this former chairman of Ethiopia's Urban Dweller's Supreme Tribunal and head of their Property Consolidation Commission fled his country. He then trekked through mine fields and enemy fire for fifteen days. Exhausting his food and water supply, he made his way across Ethiopia's border and finally to America. With deep emotion, he told me after the seminar, "I learned to forgive today—even though they took every possession I ever owned. And," he added, "God has shown me that He is going to work all of this out for my good."

But the exciting meeting with Aradam came over a year later when we met at Prison Fellowship's International Symposium at Queen's University in Belfast, Northern Ireland. After I had taught and we all had participated in "praying for those who despitefully use you," a breathless Aradam caught up with me at the elevator. "I've done it all now. I've done it! Today I was able to pray *for* them!" he beamed.

Real praying *for* a sinner must be done in love, not just from human concern or Christian duty. We can pray *about* them without loving them. But praying *for* them requires that we put our feelings and rights out of our minds and concentrate in prayer only on their needs. And the more deeply we have been hurt the greater the tendency is to pray *about* them and not *for* them. But Jesus said, "But I say to you who hear, love your enemies, do good to those who hate you, bless those who curse you, pray for those who mistreat you" (Luke 6:27–28, NASB).

By praying **with** *that sinner,* amazing strides in his or her restoration can be accomplished. Why? Together we spend time, not offering or rehearsing human counsel which may or may not be correct or timely, but interacting with the Ultimate Restorer, our Father in heaven. His answers are always true, correctly timed, and exactly right for every circumstance.

The precious hours I spent in prayer *with* that friend I was restoring were by far the most fruitful of all my efforts. Together, we lingered in His holy presence. How sweet it was just to pour out our hearts together to the Lover of our souls and feel His sweet love surround us and His powerful arms undergird us.

What happens when God answers this praying together with the repentant sinner? His restoration just seems to flow— amazingly—not only to the one being restored but also to the restorer.

Restore by loving, not legalism. So much of restoration of the repentant sinner hinges on our loving him or her. If we follow the Bible's instructions with rigid legalism, it will be perceived by this person, and our attempts at restoration may be rejected. But, if we love that one sincerely and selflessly, our actions and attitudes will be automatically supportive and restoring.

At this point, you probably are saying, "But I don't love that sinner very much. How do I get the love God wants me to have?"

One of the most effective exercises of my "What Happens When We Pray" seminars has been our praying through the scriptural formula for handling someone who has grieved us, as given in 2 Corinthians 2. Although we study it from the perspective of the responsibility of the one who has been grieved, the needs of the offender are in this portion of Scripture as well. After forgiving and promising to comfort that sinner (lest they become overwhelmed with too much sorrow), we then promise to confirm our love to him or her.

Of course, we realize that it is not possible to confirm something we don't have; so, in prayer, we ask God to give us all the love He wants us to have. Then we wait in silence after that prayer, feeling the love come from God. And it does! So, if you don't feel much love for that sinner you are restoring, get on your knees—and wait until God gives it to you.

When the repentant sinner being restored is truly loved, he or she usually responds to that love and begins the process of loving us and, even more important, himself again.

How Does God Restore the Sinner?

Humans at best can create the environment in which God can work to restore the soul. The ultimate restorer of the sinner, of course, is God. The complete work of restoring comes as He answers the plea of the repentant sinner, as when the one I was restoring finally cried out, "Father, restore my soul!"

This prayer must follow the prayer of repentance, for a forgiven soul is not the same as a restored soul. A forgiven soul is one reconciled to God, but there still may be much to be restored.

God uses Scripture to answer the prayers for restoration. "The law of the Lord is perfect, restoring the soul" (Ps. 19:7, NASB).

In the Bible verse, "All Scripture is given by inspiration of God, and is profitable for doctrine, for reproof, for correction, for instruction in righteousness" (2 Tim. 3:16), the word *correction* means "to restore to an upright state." God does restore with Scripture.

The friend I was restoring knew theologically from 1 John 1:9 that "if we [Christians] confess our sins, [God] is faithful and just to forgive us our sins, and to cleanse us from all unrighteousness" but my friend had struggled for several years trying to accept forgiveness, doing everything humanly possible to secure it. And after confessing to me, my friend still agonized for two months over God's actual forgiving. But

the reality of forgiveness came dramatically from the Bible.
It was Psalm 32 that finally did it for my friend. "Look at
this!" my friend just exploded, and slowly we read together:

How blessed is he whose transgression is forgiven,
Whose sin is covered!
How blessed is the man to whom the Lord does not impute
iniquity,
And in whose spirit there is no deceit! (vv. 1–2, NASB).

And then that oh-so-true picture of my friend's life:

When I kept silent about my sin, my body wasted away
Through my groaning all day long.
For day and night Thy hand was heavy upon me;
My vitality was drained away as with the fever-heat of summer
(vv. 3–4, NASB).

But the victory was there:

I acknowledge my sin to Thee,
And my iniquity I did not hide;
I said, "I will confess my transgressions to the Lord";
And Thou didst forgive the guilt of my sin (v. 5, NASB).

Then verse 11 produced the thrill of assurance for my friend:

"Be glad in the Lord and rejoice you righteous ones, and shout
for joy all you who are upright in heart" (Ps. 32:11, NASB).

Forgiven! Restored to an upright state! Rejoicing!
Four months later, God gave my friend, "For Thou, Lord,
art good, and ready to forgive, and abundant in lovingkindness
to all who call upon Thee" (Ps. 86:5, NASB). In the margin of
my Bible, I recorded, "My friend just opened to this today,
and took it as a personal promise!"
So God powerfully uses His written Word, the Bible, to
answer the prayer of, and for, the repentant sinner for restoration.

Forgive Yourself

But the forgiven sinner must accept God's forgiveness. How
often God cries, "I forgave you. Won't you please let Me

open the curtain to that beautiful room called 'forgiven'?"
A room filled with the sweet aroma of God's forgiveness.
Its sweetness is surprisingly pleasant, not only to the nostrils
but to the whole being. Saturating, engulfing, it completely
obliterates any lingering stench of that sin. But the response
is up to us.

A young woman who had had an abortion later married
and tried for years to become pregnant. After exhaustive medical tests and experiments, the final conclusion was—pregnancy
impossible. In the depths of despair, she cried, "I killed the
only baby I'll ever have!" How tragic to be unable to accept
God's forgiveness when there has been deep repentance. How
sad not to be able to walk once again with God in the cool
of the garden—forgiven.

God cannot restore the sinner until that sinner accepts His
forgiveness. My son-in-love, Skip, said this to me the other
day, "After God has forgiven you and you have gone to your
brother, if you can't forgive yourself, you are setting your
standards higher than God's."

The greatest enemy of restoration may be ourselves. Complete restoration can come to the repentant sinner only when
the self-loathing and the sometimes paranoid existence is exchanged for God's loving acceptance.

I sat listening to the widow of a prominent pastor who,
after sinning grievously, had committed suicide. "When he
repented deeply, the children and I forgave him, the church
forgave him, God forgave him—but," she hung her head and
sighed, "he could not forgive himself."

If Only

When there has been a devastating sin in our lives, we
say, "If only! What if I had not done it? What would I be,
what could I have accomplished if only I had not sinned?"
These are bitter words that plague the repentant sinner, causing seemingly never-ending shudders of the soul—"If only!"

To be sure, there are consequences of sinning with which
we must live. "For he who does wrong will receive the consequences of the wrong which he has done, and that without
partiality" (Col. 3:25, NASB). And again in Galatians 6:7, "Do
not be deceived, God is not mocked; for whatever a man sows,
this he will also reap" (NASB).

There will be the inevitable consequence of sin—broken relationships, ravaged bodies, a child out of wedlock, lost years the locusts have eaten. Those we will have with us always.

An emaciated, faltering young man who had found Christ after years of being on hard drugs drove up to me on his motorcycle at a youth convention and labored to say, "Mrs. Ev-e-lyn, y-y-you re-ally mi-mi-ministered to me to-to-today." Then he poured out his brokenheartedness at a body and a mind crippled for life. "If only!"

One repentant pastor cried, "Will I ever be able to have the trust and confidence of others again?"

David, even though forgiven by God, for the rest of his life paid the price for his sin against Bathsheba and her husband. God said the child she was bearing would die—and he did (2 Sam. 12:10–14). Also, David was not allowed to build the temple, and his family had to live by the sword from that time on. In his deep repentance, David often must have thought, *Oh, if only! If only I had not done it!*

Only God Restores Ministry

But, wonderfully, while we are crying "If only!" God is answering "Since." He answers our "if only" lament with, "Now then, *since* you have been forgiven, I am in charge of restoring your ministry."

David, after his deep repentance, found a very important word—*then*. Psalm 51 tells us that he bowed down acknowledging his sin, deeply repented of it, begged God to create in him a clean heart, and asked Him to restore the joy of His salvation. *"Then,"* David said, "I will teach transgressors Thy ways, and sinners will be converted to Thee" (Ps. 51:15, NASB). Restored ministry!

And incredibly, God still used that repentant, restored sinner's lineage to produce the Messiah, Jesus! The New Testament opens with these words, "The book of the genealogy of Jesus Christ, the son of David, the son of Abraham" (Matt. 1:1, NASB).

However, we must add that there is no way to know what glorious things God had planned for David had he not sinned. C. S. Lewis in his novel *Perelandra* said it like this, "Whatever you do, He will make good of it. But not the good he had prepared for you if you had obeyed Him. That is lost for ever." [1] We never will know what David's later life would have been without his horrible sin.

Many people have said to me, "God never can use me again because of that awful sin I committed." But God not only forgives when there is genuine repentance, He can restore status and position in His kingdom. We can be cleansed again for His holy ministry.

But we must remember that only God can decide if or how much ministry He will restore. We humans have nothing to do with God reinstating His call to that person. We may hire that one in a new job, or even restore his or her status in a former position, but only God can choose to once again pour out His power and blessing upon and through that one again. The decision is God's—not ours.

Peter is a tremendous example of one whose ministry was restored by God after sinning grievously. After denying his Lord the night Jesus was betrayed, Peter went out and wept bitterly. The words, "If only I had not done it," must have kept surfacing through those bitter tears. And Peter must have been convinced he was finished in the work of his Lord's kingdom.

What agony of soul Peter must have felt on that beach after the resurrection when Jesus kept asking, "Lovest thou me?" But what confusion, and then twinge of hope, must have stirred within him when Jesus said, "Feed my lambs" (John 21). In his grief, it is possible that Peter did not grasp the magnitude of Jesus' restoration of his ministry.

He was restored to ministry—shoulders back, step quickened, self-image restored, and, most important of all—a fruitful ministry for God.

But Who Restores the Restorer?

In the depths of restoring a penitent sinner, what happens when the restorer finally cries out, "Oh, Father, who restores me, the restorer?"

---

1. C. S. Lewis, *Perelandra*, © 1954 by Clive Staples Lewis (New York: Macmillan Co., 1958), p. 125.

Perhaps we have been disgraced by our teenaged child's lifestyle, devastated by a mate who has sought greener pastures, or humiliated by someone we love in Christ who is bringing shame to His holy name and ours. Does God expect us to restore that one without any concern or provision by Him for our own needs?

Since the "spiritual one" commanded to do the restoring in Galatians 6:1 is likely to be the one who has been deeply hurt by the sinning one, we ask, "Who restores the restorer?"

The Restorer Is God

I remember lifting up and praying for that one God gave me to restore for nine months. But when I was suddenly told the details of how the sinning had been against me, I felt a deep, tearing wound inside me. Then as I continued to struggle for another year in the restoring process, the burden seemed to become unbearable. And I bowed my head and sobbed, "Oh, God, who restores the restorer?"

Astonishingly, God's answer immediately filled my mind. "It's the Twenty-third Psalm," He said. Assurance flooded my soul. There it was: *"He* restoreth my soul!" God!

Restoring the restorer was part of God's original intention when He instructed us to restore the fallen one. Before telling us to "restore such a one," in Galatians 6:1, He already knew it would include His having to restore us—the restorers. Amazingly, "restore such a one" is in the continuous present Greek tense, suggesting a process of perhaps long duration, not just a once-for-all action.

Then, at the end of this portion of Scripture on restoring, God gives a promise. My heart leaped within me as I read, "And let us not lose heart in doing good, for in due time we shall reap if we do not grow weary" (Gal. 6:9, NASB).

It is admirable and tremendously helpful if the repentant sinner spends time and effort trying to make restitution to the one against whom he or she has sinned. The loving tenderness, the myriad of kind words and actions to make up for the hurting they caused are wonderful and do help so much. But the deep hole that we feel has been punched right in the middle of us only can be restored to wholeness by God.

It is only God who can fill the devastating void left by severed relationships with children, relatives, and friends and by broken marriage vows. Only God can restore the *soul*.

The Restorer's Needs

Restoring someone who has sinned can be a tremendously exhausting process. Sincerely working with, praying for, and emotionally undergirding the one who needs restoring can leave the restorer emotionally, and perhaps physically, bankrupt. There may be nothing left with which to cope.

The restorer's own self-image may have been severely damaged, especially if his or her parenting or leadership capabilities have been questioned or he or she no longer is "number one" in the eyes of the mate. Or, one may appear to be a failure when, no matter how hard you try, the sinner will not let you restore him or her. And the searching question, "Where have I failed?" seems to have no answer. So, who restores the restorer?

Also, most people tend to ignore or even be unaware of the restoration the restorer may need. It hurts when people acclaim the progress of the one being restored, but ignore the sweat, blood, and tears we have put into their recovery. Few seem to care about the hours, days, and perhaps years we have spent keeping that head above water—treading water ourselves. Nor do they seem to notice the deep wounds inflicted on us, especially if we *seem* to be strong and are "handling it beautifully."

Other people probably see only the attitudes out in public of the one being restored, while we have had to live with, and perhaps suffer in silence with, that person's mood-swinging existence, depression, self-incrimination, wrestling to admit the sin, hopelessness, and perhaps even suicidal tendencies. Others also may see their brave cover-up in public while we must live with the inevitable collapse when they reach home. So, who restores us?

Or, even worse, the hardest part is being blamed for causing the problem in that one we're trying to restore, when we know the real cause and that basically we are innocent. But because of our fierce loyalty, we are protecting that one we are restoring and will not defend ourselves by revealing the facts or order of events, when just a few words would clear our reputation.

Also, the sinning one usually sees only his or her own need, and is unaware of any need the restorer might have.

So, who restores the restorer? God says, "I will!"

When Circumstances Don't Change

Even when the circumstances don't change, and frequently they don't, God still restores us.

"Dear Evelyn," a seminar participant wrote, "I was absolutely at the end of myself. I no longer could live under the circumstances of my life. I was ready to end it all when I found your book *Lord, Change Me!* I took to heart those principles, turned to God's Word—and He restored me! My circumstances haven't changed, but my relationship with the Lord has. And He has picked me up and sent me rejoicing!" Yes, ultimately, the restoration of the restorer must be his or her relationship with God.

"My pastor-husband, who has his Ph.D. in psychology," wrote a seminar attendee, "gives away three books in counseling; and one of them is your *Lord, Change Me!* Then they let him know how the Lord is changing *them.* Even when their circumstances don't change!"

A beautiful Christian television personality shared with me her incredible restoration after her husband's suicide. He was brilliant and an extremely successful pastor, building a several-thousand-member church. "He could preach better in the flesh than most men could all prayed up," she quipped, "which, of course, was what he was doing when he fell into sin with another woman."

When he realized his church, his wife, his family, and all he was equipped to do and all he had worked for were gone, he wallowed in a pool of remorse. And finally, instead of taking the necessary steps and then accepting God's forgiveness, he committed suicide.

"We all did everything we could to restore him," she sighed sadly, searching my eyes for understanding. "But he would not let us!" But she had let God restore her!

Although crushed and devastated, this beautiful woman was able to turn to God and receive the strength to sustain her and her family through it all. Now she not only has been restored by God but she also has a nationwide ministry to hurting singles.

When the mother of her teenage daughter's friend collapsed and had a nervous breakdown under similar circumstances, this restored woman's daughter said, "Thanks, Mom, for being a godly woman!"

Let God Be God

Don't expect other people to be your only source of restoration. Don't depend on your pastor, your mate, your family, or friends to fill all your lonely hours and the devastating void. Let God be God in your life.

How can I be restored to being the loving restorer when attitudes surface in me such as, "I'd rather retract my hand than touch," "I'd rather run away than walk beside," or, "I'd rather throw in the towel than pick up the apron"? Who can handle these negative feelings in me? God—as He restores my soul!

Give God a chance. Spend at least as much time with Him as with others to whom you are clinging for support. A woman whose husband had left her called again last week, saying she was so confused by all the conflicting instructions and advice different people were giving her.

"Stop talking to people for a while," I replied. "Instead, keep taking your Bible and reading it until God speaks to you. Then stop reading and talk to the Author of that Book— God. See what advice and comfort He has for you. Then you will have what is true and also what is right for you at the moment."

People Also Restore the Restorer

God also uses people to answer our prayer, "Who restores the restorer?"

People can play a huge part in restoring the restorer by undergirding, listening, understanding, supporting, and spending time with them. Even when they don't know why the restorer needs restoring, they frequently are sensitive enough to that hurting one to give their needed support.

The Christian church is intended to be a place, not where we ignore, gossip, and criticize, but where we restore our hurting ones. Immediately following the instructions to restore the sinner, in Galatians 6:1, we are told to "bear one another's burdens" (v. 2, NASB). One of the important ways to do this is by taking time to affirm others through our caring and support.

I watched my own church obey this admonition as our members flocked around a beautiful wife who was struggling to restore her wandering husband. Sometimes, it was a squeeze or a handshake while our eyes met hers with an affirming, "I understand," "We're with you all the way," or, "Hang in there!" Sometimes, we helped with a myriad of little and big actions needed to fill the empty moments, lonely prayer times, missed conversations—or even financial needs.

But the most important way relatives and friends can restore the restorer is to pray for that struggling one. Here, too, prayer releases God's healing balm on the wounds, His strength for sagging knees, and His courage to the fainting heart. A letter arrived one day from a woman who asked why God woke her nightly for the past two weeks to pray for me. Another day, a member of our Twin Cities metropolitan prayer chain, whom I'd never met and who was totally unaware of the kind of prayer I needed, told me that she has been rising at 3:00 o'clock every morning to pray for me. Many times, I have been acutely aware that without all their prayers I never would have made it.

When I left a luncheon in Fort Worth, Texas, during my period of devastation, a former missionary to Korea evidently sensed my need, squeezed me, and told me she would pray for me during my trip home. Oh, how I could sense those prayers. And I felt myself taking a huge step forward in my own restoration on the plane.

His Answers to Our Prayers

Perhaps the greatest way God restores us, the restorers, is to answer our own prayers for help.

I had prayed, "Lord, heal me!" for several days during my time of restoring my friend. But it was on a Saturday morning after a long dry spell without rain in our city, and then two days of refreshing rain, that I was sitting on our deck and asking Him to heal me again. I was just waiting quietly in

His presence, in that washed air as the birds sang, and my heart suddenly soared. I was thrilled as I let the warm sun and the Son relax me, fill and thrill my whole being. My eyes were moist with teardrops of thanks and love for God! I felt Him streaming into me—as real as the warm, morning sun. I brushed away a stray tear of joy that crept down my cheek. God!!!

This was just one of a long series of answers to my original prayer, "God, who restores me, the restorer?" But I have learned I must allow Him to restore me. There is a law involved here: The speed and completeness of my restoration is determined by what I let God do in me as He answers this prayer.

But there is another kind of prayer. A member of the Godhead is praying for me, the restorer. One day during my prayer time, I was feeling the brunt of Satan's attacks and was emotionally drained. Then a smile spread across my face as I suddenly envisioned Jesus praying for me—sitting up there at the right hand of the Father, interceding for me! "He always lives to make intercession for them" (Heb. 7:25, NASB). I thanked Him with great joy in my heart as I asked Him to continue the praying He started in His high-priestly prayer, "[Father], keep them from the evil one" (John 17:15, NASB).

The Enemy of Restoration

Why did Jesus pray that prayer just before leaving earth? And why did He teach us, His followers, to pray, "[Father] . . . deliver us from the evil one" (Matt. 6:13, NASB), in His model Lord's Prayer? Because Jesus knew how our enemy Satan would operate, trying to negate God's will on earth just as he had tried in heaven before God cast him out. The battle is a spiritual one as Satan desires to thwart God's restoration.

There will continue to be times when places, things, and people remind both the restorer and the one being restored of the sin. Painful memories flash in the mind as they pass the building or city in which the sin took place, when they suddenly are face to face with the person with whom the sin was committed, or pass nearby but are unobserved by that person—initiating renewed grief or remorse.

At one such time, I was engulfed in past hurts, and the

friend I was restoring was in deep sorrow because of the hurt caused me. The next day as we were talking through this devastating experience, my friend asked, "How do you handle these flashbacks? How come you have victory, but I don't? The only way I can handle them is finally just to dismiss them. I am able to agonize in the remorse and regrets just so long, and then I have to put them out of my mind—and get very, very busy filling my mind so I won't think about it anymore."

As I pondered the reason, I suddenly was aware that I did have victory already the next day. I had returned to a state of peace and even joy in that short time. "I think the difference is that, rather than dismiss them, I handle my feelings," I replied. When my friend asked how, I explained the steps.

"First, recognize the source of these flashbacks. Satan is the enemy of restoration. The last thing he wants is for the one he has trapped in a deep sin to be restored. (Of course, God, too, may have reasons for bringing warnings and teaching through His recalling.)

"So, instead of dismissing my feelings," I continued, "I flee to my prayer closet. Yesterday, I spent an hour and a half with the Lord praying this through. Then I echoed Jesus' intercession for me, 'Father, deliver me from the evil one, Satan.'

"The next step," I explained, "is not prayer, but addressing Satan himself. With unshakable faith in Jesus' finished work on the cross and the resultant power of His blood, I tell Satan I'm claiming this blood against him. I even visualize that irresistible force of Jesus' shed blood rushing through my body and my mind, dislodging Satan and sweeping all of his influences right out of me.

"I then ask God to forgive me for all my negative thoughts and however I have let Satan have the upper hand in my thoughts as I succumbed to his fiery memory dart.

"The next step is asking God the Holy Spirit to fill me with Himself. The vacuum that has been created in me by God emptying and forgiving me," I concluded, "needs to be filled with Him."

And God does it! Peace, His positive thoughts, His stability inside me like a solid rock. Victory is there! And, incredibly, there is love in me for the one who sinned against me—renewed and reinforced—and even enlarged.

Elva Stump, a ninety-seven-year-old who was at our Lakeland, Florida, seminar, stood and gave us all her secrets for such a long and victorious life. "Because Jesus loves me and I love Him, I keep filled with the Holy Spirit. First, Jesus helps me to love everybody, and pray for the unlovely, for their salvation. Second, He helps me to hold no grudges or resentment. Confession and forgiveness are a must. Third, He helps me to reject negative thoughts. The devil uses our minds as his playground—if we let him. So, reject the first negative thought. How do you do this? Discipline, and work at it!"

So, instead of Satan cackling his hideous laugh of victory, chalking up one more Christian having "bitten the dust," he retreats, whipped, his prey snatched from his grasp.

And the kingdom of God marches on—victorious, restored, powerful, and conquering—just as God intended it to do. This is not without struggles and battles, but with His children taking seriously the mandate from Him to restore the repentant sinner—and to be restored themselves!

"Lest You, Too"

There is a warning for the restorer in the portion of Galatians 6 about the spiritual ones restoring the one caught in a sin. While reading this Scripture in a recent "Lord, Change Me" seminar, God stopped me on the words, "Looking to yourself lest you too be tempted" (v. 1, NASB).

"Lord," I prayed, "search my heart *lest* I be tempted too. Search me *before* I am. Oh, God, what kind of temptation will it be? Surely not the same kind. I've never had those thoughts. Oh, God, what kind of temptation?"

Then, shocked, I cried, "Is that the answer in verse 3? 'For if anyone thinks he is something when he is nothing, he deceives himself.' The sin of pride? Thinking I am greater than the one I'm restoring? Oh, God, forgive me! I already have been tempted to think too much of myself."

Reverse That Trend

As my friend and I talked about all the leading Christian national and even international musicians, writers, and pastors who had fallen into sin, I said, "What we really need to break this insidious trend in Christian leadership today is for one of them—one of the famous ones—to repent publicly. Perhaps on radio or TV or in a national magazine to call it what it is—sin—and ask the Christian community to forgive him or her. Then promise to do everything possible to make restitution for all the shattered trust in their leadership.

"Maybe if just one would do it," I continued, "it would give Christians a chance to obey the scriptural commands to forgive and restore that penitent sinner. Give us a chance, not to cancel their appearances in our churches and their concerts, not to take their books off our shelves or programs off Christian radio and TV stations—but to forgive when God forgives.

"This would give all those hundreds, thousands, and even millions following their leadership not only the right to see their hero or heroine's error in their sinning and their unworthiness to be followed, but it would also be a courageous example of what God expects from and will do for the followers if they sin."

The problem is, we all have a tendency to want to be restored without paying the price. We expect to jump from our gross sins right back to ministry, fellowship, and respect. We have convinced ourselves that, when we pray, "Lord, I have sinned," only restoration is necessary—while God is insisting on repentance, reconciliation, and restitution first.

Rest

Amazingly, when these scriptural instructions have been obeyed and applied, and the seemingly endless struggles and hurts finally are past, the end result of that restoration is found in its first four letters—R-E-S-T.

But it is only when we obediently have followed all the steps of repentance, reconciliation, restitution, and allowing God to restore us that we experience His ultimate for us—*rest:* that beautiful state free from guilt, estrangement, and burdens. Only then are we able to relax in the joy of unbroken fellowship with God and others.

The process producing enmity, anger, and wounds has been reversed. And Satan, defeated, goes slinking offstage while

God pulls the curtain open on a new era in our lives—peace with Him, with others, and with ourselves. Restored!

Closing Prayer

Father, teach me Your steps in the restoration process. Help me to examine where I am in all my relationships with others. Make me aware of how I am hurting them, and help me correct it. Make me a restorer to those who need me. Take my hurts from other people and in Your time, and in Your way, restore me to perfect oneness with them and to perfect rest in You.

In Jesus' name, **Amen.**

11

WHEN GOD ANSWERS . . .

Now Obey Me

What happens when God answers? What God always expects to happen—our *obedience*.

After God has answered our prayer, whether exciting, mind-boggling, or difficult, the next step is obedience. When God answers our prayer with a command, instruction, or an open door, He fully expects us to obey. We must put into practice what God has told us in His answer. And our obedience to His answer to our prayer opens the curtain on the next act of our lives. "So shall my word be which goes forth from my mouth, it shall not return to me empty, without accomplishing what I desire, and without succeeding in the matter for which I sent it" (Isa. 55:11, NASB).

This is the God of the universe speaking, the One whom all the stars, planets, weather, and seasons obey. The One who spoke, and the universe came into being. The One who spoke, and the sea was calm. Who spoke, and the dead came alive. The One who expects obedience to His words.

However, God does not coerce us into obeying His answers to our prayers. He has given each of us a free will, with the privilege of responding as we choose. And, astoundingly, we humans frequently ignore, rebel, make excuses, refuse to obey, or even laugh at a certain answer from Him. This is amazing in light of the fact that it is the omniscient God of the universe who has answered us.

Our son, Kurt, said it to me this way: "Remember, when dealing with the Great Potter, the quality of the pot is solely determined by the malleability of the clay." It is our ability and willingness as clay to obey and be shaped by God, the Potter, that ultimately fashions what we are—and what God can do through us.

What Are You Missing?

Have you ever wondered what you have missed in life because of a wrong response to God's directions?

For years, I have wondered what Jesus' disciples missed on the day of His resurrection because of disobedience. How had Jesus planned to return in His risen body to that little grieving, disillusioned band? What kind of joyous reunion did He have in mind for them?

Somehow, I feel Jesus had planned a jubilant, victorious appearance—turning their shattering grief into instantaneous rejoicing. Celebrating in Galilee, rather than hiding in Jerusalem. Galilee—where He could reveal Himself—alive and victorious over sin and death. What a reunion! Their crucified leader, risen from the dead—suddenly in their midst!

Jesus had instructed His disciples twice to go to Galilee and meet Him there; but, because of their wrong response to His words, they missed what He evidently had planned for them.

First, before His death, Jesus had given them instructions as to where He would go and that they should follow, saying, "But after I have been raised, I will go *before you* into Galilee" (Matt. 26:32, NASB). But instead of obeying Him after His death, their response to this instruction was to hide in fear behind locked doors in Jerusalem, thereby missing the planned reunion in Galilee.

The second time the disciples' response was wrong was on Easter morning before Jesus had appeared to any of them. The angel and Jesus Himself both sent word to them through the women at the tomb:

And the angel answered and said to the women, "Do not be afraid; for I know that you are looking for Jesus who has been crucified. He is not here, for He has risen: . . . And go quickly and tell His disciples that He has risen from the dead; and behold, *He is going before you into Galilee; there you will see Him."*. . . And they departed quickly from the tomb with fear and great joy, and ran to report it to His disciples. And behold, Jesus met them and greeted them. And they came up and took hold of His feet and worshiped Him. Then Jesus said to them, "Do not be afraid; go and take word to My brethren *to leave for Galilee, and there they shall see Me"* (Matt. 28:5–10, NASB, emphasis mine).

Mark, in his Gospel, tells us that the angel at the empty tomb even reminded the women of Jesus' command, "Go tell His disciples and Peter, He is going before you into Galilee; there you will see Him, *just as He said unto you"* (Mark 16:7, NASB, emphasis mine).

This time, the disciples' wrong response was *unbelief.* Luke tells us that "these words appeared to them as nonsense, and they would not believe them" (Luke 24:11, NASB). Words telling them that Jesus was alive! Words telling them that they still could have that reunion in Galilee!

So Jesus had to settle for second best. And the reunion that had to take place in Jerusalem was so much less than He had hoped. When Jesus finally did appear to the disciples, they were huddled behind locked doors, "startled and frightened and thought they were seeing a spirit" (Luke 24:37, NASB).

Also, after Jesus appeared to the two on the Emmaus Road, they hurried back to tell the grieving disciples. But Mark tells us they did not believe them either. "And afterward [after appearing to the women and the two], He appeared to the eleven themselves as they were reclining at table, and *He reproached them* for their unbelief and hardness of heart, because they had not believed those who had seen Him after He had risen" (Mark 16:14, NASB). Reproach instead of triumph!

How disappointed Jesus must have been. His return to His disciples after His death and resurrection filled them with fear, mourning, weeping, unbelief, and fright. They even had to be scolded by their beloved Master. His plans for the greatest moment of their lives were ruined—all because they refused to believe and obey His words.

Perhaps there are excuses for their disobedience—they forgot Jesus' words, they didn't understand in the first place, or they were too grieved to think rationally. But even when the angel prodded their memories by sending the message "as He told *you*" with the women, their response was still unbelief and disobedience.

Then, their response, even when Jesus Himself sent a personal message to them, was seemingly inexcusable—unbelief. Was it their hopelessness, their grief? Was it their view of the messengers—women, unfit to be witnesses in those days? Yet, the women were entrusted by both the angel and Jesus with "He is risen"—the most significant piece of information ever to be released on planet earth!

Yes, the only ones who didn't miss the glorious impact of that first Easter were the women and the two on the Emmaus Road. The rest missed the greatest opportunity ever offered to mankind. A mind-exploding reunion with their supposedly dead leader—the risen, triumphant, glorified Lord! Oh, what might have been!

It was only when the disciples finally did go "to Galilee, to the mountain which Jesus had designated" (Matt. 28:16, NASB), that they received their marching orders for the future—the Great Commission.

I wonder how many of my Galilees I have missed? Missed because I'm aghast at the prospect of a cross, too grieved to see clearly, or have an inadequate view of the Messenger, my Lord. Missed because of unbelief, disobedience. Missed because of not responding to a simple, seemingly unimportant little piece of instruction like, "Go to Galilee, and there I will meet you." Oh, what my today might have been had all my responses to my Lord been belief and obedience!

What are you missing that Jesus had planned for you? Joy, hope, peace? An intimate walk with Jesus? Renewed fellowship with Him? Are you living like the disciples—in despair, defeat, fear, tears, unbelief, and disobedience? Then it is because your response to His words also has been wrong. Perhaps you are feeling that there are good reasons why you should not believe and obey. But the hard fact is that you are missing the triumphant, joyous relationship with Him that He is longing to have with you—if you were obedient.

"Just Trust Me!"

What God actually is saying to us when He gives us commands, directions, and open doors is, "Just trust Me!" In return, what response does He expect from us to His "Just trust Me"? Just trusting Him!

There are three kinds of people: those irresponsible beings who eat, drink, and are "merry" for tomorrow they may die; those who perpetually worry about what might happen; and those who live in that wonderful state of trusting God. Those who have learned to take the hassle out of their lives by casting all their cares on Him—and then relaxing in Him.

The air controllers had gone on strike the day I was due in Oklahoma City. I was told by an airline official, "Lady, we can get you as far as Dallas, but there's absolutely nothing going out of there to Oklahoma City." I could almost feel the quizzical look on his face as I replied, "OK, I'll take your plane as far as Dallas."

With mixed emotions, my executive director, Sally, took me to the airport and deposited me with a waiting skycap. Then she returned home to pray. She and Jeanne, her prayer partner, added their prayers to those of the telephone prayer chain already asking God to intervene in a humanly hopeless situation, as I was due to start speaking that afternoon at a denominational annual meeting in Oklahoma City.

When Sally and Jeanne finished praying, they looked at each other and confidently giggled, "I wonder how God is going to get Ev out of *this* one?"

Unaware of their spirit of expectant confidence in God, I couldn't wait to get off that plane in Dallas to see what God was going to do. It never dawned on me that He might not have a solution. For years, in answer to multiplied prayers, I had practiced an abandonment to God that produced such exciting results. There was not even a twinge of doubt that God had His plan all worked out.

As I walked the Dallas Airport jet-way from the plane to the terminal, my chest was almost bursting with exhilaration. I felt like a young colt, nostrils slightly flared in anticipation, tail flying high, prancing into a challenging headwind.

But I was not prepared for what I saw in that terminal. Even though I'd missed a plane once and had been stranded overnight in this new mega airport, I was stunned. Baggage was piled high everywhere. Stranded passengers of all sizes, races, and financial means were sprawled, trying to sleep with heads propped on baggage. Some just sat dejectedly, while others wended their way over and through the people and suitcases hoping to find some way to go some place.

A long makeshift row of airline ticket booths had been set up for agents to try to assist the almost hopeless sea of passengers. They herded us into a long line, and as openings occurred, they sent each one to the next available official.

My agent looked at me and said, "Lady, there's *nothing* going to Oklahoma City any time today." I nodded my understanding. "Except . . . that man who just left my booth. He's around that corner trying to make a telephone call to see if there is a car he can rent to drive to Oklahoma City. Of course, all the cars have been gone for hours. But if you hurry you should catch him just as he comes back around that corner—" His voice trailed off as I dashed away.

Then I did something I've never done before—or since. With absolute assurance in my heart that it was right, I rushed up to that unknown man and gasped, "Are you going to Oklahoma City?" His startled response was, "Well, I, ah, my wife and I are." Then with an incredulous expression on his face, he explained that, just as he made that call someone canceled a car reservation and rather than checking the whole reservation mess, they just gave it to him.

He led me to his weary wife, propped up on their baggage, both protecting it and trying to get a little rest. While he went to get the car, his wife and I exchanged pleasantries. "Oh, you are going to a convention, too? That's nice. In the same hotel I'll be in? How interesting. Your husband is what? Eastern director for the Holiness Association? Oh, that's the convention where I'm going to speak!" We hugged and laughed, amazed at our God's incredible working.

Her husband returned with the car, and we set out walking those long terminals trying to get a glimpse of my luggage. Just as a porter put his hand on my suitcase to "store it who knows where?" we just happened to be walking by! Another miracle.

We missed the first session, along with almost everybody else; but on the way, our car was filled with praise and gratitude as we pieced together God's plan. And joy and laughter filled our hearts. "Just trust Me!"

But, Can God Trust You?

Are you secretly longing to get out of your status quo and into something you think would be more glamorous, more important for the Lord? The secret of God being able to do greater things through us is found in 1 Corinthians 4:2, "It is required of stewards that they be found trustworthy" (NASB).

Stewards are those to whom something has been entrusted for which they are responsible and accountable. In the Bible, stewards include the manager of a household, a governor of young children, an official of a city, elders and bishops in the church, and those entrusted with the mysteries of God. Each of us has been entrusted with differing gifts from God— a household, children, a civic position, work in the church, money, and the mysteries of God—making us all stewards. And according to God's Word, stewards are required to be faithful—trustworthy.

So how can being a steward determine whether or not God can trust us with bigger things? Our track record. Jesus said, "He that is faithful in a very little thing is faithful also in much" (Luke 16:10, NASB). So it is he who is faithful over a few things who can be entrusted with greater things. We demonstrate our faithfulness and trustworthiness by what we have done with what God has given us in the past.

Jesus explained this in His parable of the talents in Matthew 25. The servants to whom the Master entrusted the five and two talents (money) each doubled them for Him. It didn't matter how many talents had been entrusted to each for, upon returning, the Master commended them both by saying, "Well done, thou good and faithful servant" (v. 21).

The Master did *not* add, "You have been faithful over a few things—so go on vacation and rest." Nor, "You have been faithful over a few things—so you deserve an early retirement." No. Instead, He said a shocking thing, "Now I will make you ruler over many." When the Master found the steward faithful, He gave him a bigger job to do.

Frequently, I am asked, "How can I do something great for God?" Or, "I have this fabulous idea; how can I write a million-copy book?" And surprisingly, these questions often are asked by someone not involved in serving Christ in any way. God knows if He can trust us with a bigger job by what we are doing right now with that seemingly insignificant or monotonous task.

Only when we are obeying His answers to our previous prayers will God open bigger and wider doors of service.

He Will Do It—If He Calls

Since God expects us to trust Him and obey Him, what, in turn, can we expect of Him? That God fully expects to do it through us! It is in those times when I honestly respond, "Lord, I can't," that He answers, "No, you can't. But I can— and will."

Discovering our God-given gifts and talents is good, but there is one more step: obeying when God calls us into a job we feel sure we do not have the gifts or talent for. This is stepping out on faith. But, of course, this is only done when we are positive that God has specifically called us. And then He will do it through us.

It was the first Sunday night of April 1981, and the next morning I was to participate in my first Prison Fellowship national board meeting with Charles Colson. I knelt struggling in prayer in my motel room in Washington, D.C., telling the Lord how incapable I felt, how I was not smart enough to be on that board, how I was not able to do the job. Feelings of total inadequacy swept over my being as I continued there in prayer crying, "God, I can't."

Finally I asked God for some Scripture so that I would have *His* words for me. I turned to 1 Thessalonians 5, where I was in my daily devotional reading. And there it was, verse 24: "Faithful is He who calls you, and He also will bring it to pass" (NASB). The King James translation says, "He will do it!"

The answer exploded within me. *I* don't have to do it. God will! *I* don't have to be all those things I know I can't be. *I* don't have to do those things I know I can't do. God will do them through me.

But then I wondered, am I eligible for God to be faithful in performing that prison board task? He had promised to be faithful only when *He* had called me to a task, when it was *His* voice I was obeying. Carefully I reviewed His call.

Three years before, while I was standing silently and alone in Fellowship House in Washington, God unexpectedly had said "prison ministry" to me. It was almost as if a mantle had dropped out of heaven and wrapped around me as He spoke. And I had simply and immediately told Him I would go—if He opened the door. Yes, I knew that I had been called by Him, and so I was eligible for Him to do it. Just as He had done it in the prisons where I had ministered—when I didn't know how—those three intervening years.

I jotted a note in the margin of my Bible by 1 Thessalonians 5:24, "God's answer, The joy and excitement are here." My attitude completely changed from apprehension to joy because I had received God's answer promising that He didn't expect *me* to do it, *He* would! How about you? Are there many times, as with me, when you wallow in a mire of self-doubts, feelings of inadequacy, unworthiness?

In our prayer seminars, just before confessing sins aloud to God, I read a list of Scripture verses with questions. After reading Ephesians 3:20, "Now unto *him* that is able to do exceeding abundantly above all that we ask or think, according to the power that worketh in us," I follow with these questions: "Do you fail to attempt things for God because you are not talented or wise enough?" "Do feelings of inferiority keep you from trying to serve God?" A yes answer, according to God in James 4:17, is a sin that needs to be confessed.

If it is true in your life today that you feel you are not talented or wise enough to serve God, confess it as sin and accept His promise that, if *He* has called you, *He* will do it!

Expect Him to Do It

At the first seminar series I did in England in 1981, I said to my husband, "This is the first place I feel their expectancy exceeds mine. I usually am the one who gets the vision and motivates others. But there is an unbelievable spiritual hunger and expectancy here."

I was baffled as they introduced me at times "for such a day as this." But they then told me it was because of their taking seriously the turn-of-the-century predictions by a Russian monk recorded in a current best seller. He had predicted that Germany would be divided in two, France would lose her power, Italy would be devastated by natural disasters, Britain would lose her empire and all her colonies, and would be on the brink of disaster—all of which to that time had come true. But the last part of England's prediction was that she would be saved by her praying women.

Sensing the magnitude of it all, I knelt in my morning devotional time in a motel in Plymouth, England, overlooking the bay from which the Pilgrims had sailed for America. It was the day of my first full seminar in the British Isles, and I asked God to bring to my mind any sin that I needed to confess, that would hinder Him from working in my audiences there. Immediately His answer shot into my mind—stark, singular—"UNBELIEF!"

Stunned and bewildered, I started questioning Him—almost in self-defense. "Lord, am I not the one who flew to Taiwan all alone, completely trusting You for safety, strength, and power in ministry? God, didn't I give You my body in 1965 and haven't had an anxious thought about it since then? Lord, don't You remember that when I lost the use of my left leg for a while I never once questioned Your wisdom or purpose? Father, don't You remember how in Florida this spring when that infection went into my bloodstream, with complete faith in You, I got out of bed and taught that all-day seminar? Father, You know that I not only teach absolute faith in the God who never makes a mistake—but also believe it—and live it. Don't You, God?"

God patiently waited for me to finish defending myself and then clearly brought His answer to my mind. "Yes, all those things are true. However, that is *obedience*. But—" The silence of His pause was deafening. "But," He finally continued, "you do not have enough *faith in what I am going to do* when you are obedient. You aren't thinking big enough!"

After I had begged God to forgive me and then waited silently before Him in prayer, He again recalled my favorite "faith" verse for me, the one He had used for years to enlarge my faith—Hebrews 11:6. "But without faith it is impossible to please [God]."

Our daughter, Nancy, had much greater expectations when she wrote on my birthday card, "Dear Mom: Your 58th year brought us the Churchwoman of the Year, your millionth copy of *What Happens When Women Pray* and many fabulous seminars all over the world. I can't wait to see what God does for an encore during your 59th year! Love, Nancy." But to me, it was God who kept saying, "You still haven't discovered what I will do when you are obedient!"

Yes, our obedience needs faith. It takes faith to submit totally to His will and then more faith to step out in obedience. Not faith in our own faith—as it sometimes is—but faith in God and who He is. The omniscient God who, with more than four billion people on planet earth, can give each His undivided attention all the time—while keeping a running total of all past actions, motives, and the outcome of all the current action. This is our God.

You Haven't Finished the Task Yet

Obedience is not just an occasional burst of obeying God. The apostle John wrote in 1 John 3:22 that we have power in prayer "because we keep His commandments and do the things that are pleasing in His sight" (NASB). And the words *keep* and *do* are in continuous tenses, meaning that we keep on keeping His commandments and doing the things that please Him.

Obedience is ongoing, not just one quick act. It involves stick-to-it-iveness, tenaciously persevering as long as God does not withdraw the call or command.

The first night of our International Prayer Assembly in Seoul, Korea, God reminded me powerfully to "take heed to the ministry which you have received in the Lord, that you may *fulfill* it" (Col. 4:17, NASB).

Then, at the end of that summer, I was feeling emotionally and physically exhausted, and I was reluctant to keep going full time with seminars and writing, plus my new grandbabies and such a full family life. I even had discussed with my husband how I might pull back.

For that September's United Prayer Ministries annual retreat, God had directed me to use Revelation 2 and 3. As I was preparing from these chapters, He abruptly spoke to me out of 3:2, "Wake up, and strengthen the things that remain, which were about to die; for I have not found your deeds complete in the sight of My God" (NASB).

You may think you are done, Evelyn, but God doesn't see your task completed. He is not finished with you yet!

"My Door, Not Yours"

It was at that retreat when we were reading individually Revelation 2 and 3, seeking His direction for the future of our organization, that God reminded me that it was *His* door, not mine, through which our prayer ministry had gone.

I still was having feelings of "throwing in the towel," or at least part of it, when God spoke to me dramatically through Revelation 3:7. In 1967, it was Revelation 3:8 that He used to call me to my prayer ministry, "Behold, I have set before [you] an open door." So the verse preceding it shocked me; and for the first time, I saw the whole picture. It is Jesus "who opens and no one will shut," and also Jesus "who shuts and no one will open."

Who did I think I was, deciding whether or not to shut or at least partially shut a door that wasn't even mine? When the Lord opens a door, no human has the right to shut it; but also, when He shuts it, no person has the power to open it.

As we met back together to pray aloud about what God had told us in the Scripture reading, I wept as I confessed before the others, "Please, Father, forgive me for looking only at myself, my weariness, my life too full of the tyranny of the urgent, and how old I'm getting. I have taken my eyes off the One who opened the door, Jesus. Forgive me for seeing it as my door. Oh, not my door, Jesus—Your door!"

Waiting

One of the most difficult parts of obedience is waiting. It almost seems like seeing the flash of His lightning, and having only to wait and wait for the boom of the thunder of His power, accomplishing what He called us to do.

There are two kinds of waiting for answers to our prayers. First, there is the kind where we wait in His presence until He answers. We practice this in our prayer seminars while praying through the 2 Corinthians 2 forgiving formula. I ask all to pray aloud in their groups of four for God's love for the one they just forgave. Then I request that they wait—in silence—until they feel that love come. And it is amazing how we can feel God's love just descending on all of us— answering immediately, while we wait.

I do this same waiting personally in my daily devotions. Before each seminar or speaking engagement, I always pray, "Lord, fill me for today." And many times, the answer comes immediately with the warm, powerful filling for that day's ministry. But it does not always come so quickly. Sometimes, even after exhausting all the requirements in my life that need to be prayed through, I finally pray, "Lord, I will not rise from my knees until You bless me! I will not even take time to eat breakfast before this huge day if You don't bless me!" Then I wait on my knees, often struggling in prayer, for His answer until it comes. This is like Jacob wrestling at the Jabbok River, not letting go until God had granted his request.

But there is a second kind of waiting for answers to our prayers in which we must give God much more time to answer. We must pray and trust in His sovereignty while we wait for Him to answer—in His timing. But this waiting sometimes is spent persisting in prayer; and other times, God assures us that we have done our part and can release it to Him. But it is always waiting—hours, days, or perhaps even years.

The Bible is full of accounts of those called by God who waited for Him to carry out their commitment. Moses' heart burned within him to rescue his people from their taskmasters in Egypt, but God sent him to the backside of the desert for forty years before consummating that call into action.

Paul, also, after receiving his dramatic call on the road to Damascus obeyed God's instructions to "rise, and enter the city, and it shall be told you what you must do" (Acts 9:6, NASB), waited for three days, blind and neither eating nor drinking. He waited until God sent Ananias to lay his hands on him, to have his sight restored, and to be filled with the Holy Spirit. Then Paul was ready for the ministry to which God had called him.

Even Jesus, after His resurrection, told His followers that they had to wait before they could bring this earth-shaking news to the world. So, after His ascension, for ten whole days, they waited—in prayer. Waited for His Pentecost promise of power!

Obedience Is Born in the Closet

Obedience is born not while purchasing a plane ticket or enrolling in a school, but in the closet—the prayer closet.

As I communicate with God in prayer for guidance, He answers with His plans and goals for me. And the way I respond in submission to Him determines the extent and depth of my obedience. It is in the prayer closet that I do my deciding, resolving, promising—and then make plans to work them out in the corporate board meeting, committee meeting, or with my family.

I set all my life's goals in my prayer closet. This not only makes them a joint project between God and me, but they actually are not my goals at all—but God's for me. Then, when I pray in obedience making His goals my goals, He goes to work fulfilling them—because they are His will.

The goals I set without including God so often fail because, though they seem like such good goals, they may not be God's will for me. Then, of course, He will not bring them to pass.

Also, human goals so frequently fizzle or are forgotten like New Year's resolutions. But never God's goals! He is only looking for willing and obedient people through whom He can accomplish His goals for this world.

Not Doing?

One of the most difficult aspects of obedience is being willing *not* to do something. Obedience isn't only going and doing, it also is *not* going and *not* doing. This is especially hard when we feel that the job or activity is so right and so necessary.

There is an important step to take in most major tasks to which I feel God is calling me. After the excitement and emotional thrill have died down, I pray a different kind of prayer: "Lord, I give this back to You—not to do it—if that is Your will." These are not just mouthed words but a total submission of my whole being to what He wants.

This prayer helps avoid many wrong turns on the road of life. It eliminates much overextending of ourselves in doing things which humanly seem so right, but can be disastrous to His plans for us. Jeremiah said it so well, "For I know the plans that *I* have for you, declares the Lord, plans for welfare and not for calamity to give you a future and a hope" (29:11, NASB).

Paul must have been surprised and even confused when the Spirit did not permit him to speak the Word to those in Asia when he was so convinced that they needed to hear of

Jesus. But God's plan was so right, and Paul's obedience opened Europe to the gospel.

Also, when a position or job would bring prestige, honor, and favorable exposure to the world, it is especially hard to release it back to God. But, when we are willing to decrease so that He and His kingdom may increase—this is real obedience.

Surprisingly for me, it frequently is *only* after I have prayed that prayer of release that God flings the door open wide to what He originally called me to do. To God, my complete obedience seems to include being willing not to do it; and then He says, "Now go!"

The Price

Obedience, also, does not mean that we are always thrilled about going to some exciting or perhaps exotic place to share Jesus. Real obedience is going when it hurts.

My obedience has been deeply tested in relation to my grandbabies. Our Nancy was long overdue with her Kathleen this fall, overlapping the start of my fall speaking schedule with her birth. So while Nancy was in the hospital delivering her baby, I was boarding a plane for an out-of-state seminar. I desperately wanted to be near my daughter, and the price of obedience loomed high. My heart ached as I flew farther and farther from her, praying through every step of that birth. The minute I arrived in Omaha, I phoned the recovery room, and the first sound I heard was the cry of my new granddaughter—too far away to hold in my arms or even to see. But Jesus said, "He who loves son or daughter more than Me is not worthy of Me" (Matt. 10:37, NASB).

When it was time for me to leave for India in 1982, my heart was heavy over being gone for five weeks while my new grandbabies were being bonded to their paternal grandmothers. We had waited ten years for these first grandchildren, and our two daughters delivered just five weeks apart.

But while reading in Luke 14 between Cindy's and Jennifer's births, God stopped me on Jesus' words in verse 33, "So therefore, no one of you can be My disciple who *does not give up all his own possessions*" (NASB). And I knew that the words *give up* literally meant "bid farewell to."

"Lord," I prayed, "does that include grandbabies?" And His yes answer sent me to my knees, weeping. I struggled long over having empty arms at leaving tiny Cindy, and perhaps the right to even see my other grandchild before I left for India.

Drying my tears, I read on into Luke 15. Jesus was speaking again, "I tell you that in the same way, there will be more joy in heaven over one sinner who repents, than over ninety-nine righteous persons who need no repentance" (v. 7, NASB).

A new prayer emerged, "Oh, God, *replace* the joy of holding my newborn babes in my arms with the joy of a sinner coming to Christ in India." Then I changed my prayer to, "No, Lord, *many sinners!*"

I wrote to each of those wee ones from India, "God has answered Grandma's prayer. Thousands have prayed here, making sure they have a personal relationship with Jesus." And God had drawn back the curtain of heaven, and let me glimpse the angels, also rejoicing over lost ones finding Christ.

But that was not the only joy I found in obeying God by going to India. The sixth night there, I was struck with severe diarrhea. The next day, I spoke shakily from 8:00 A.M. to 8:30 P.M., with Chris taking just two of the hours. I finished the last two hours physically propped up because my muscles suddenly were quivering like jelly from a pill a doctor gave me right there on the platform for the terrible pain in my stomach. Then, the very next morning, I woke with all the symptoms of a respiratory infection. However, instead of fear and panic at the possibility of becoming too sick to carry on the heavy schedule before me, I relaxed in God's unbelievable joy that engulfed me and bubbled up from within.

In my diary, I described it "as tiny, soft droplets spraying tenderly from a fountain somewhere within me in that parched and dusty city." Asking God for a word to describe that rare and extraordinary joy, He immediately brought to my mind *effusive.* Back home, my dictionary defined effusive as "pouring out, overflowing, lacking reserve like effusive greetings or an effusive person, unrestrained. . . ." Exactly what my sick body was feeling that morning in India—effusive, overflowing, unrestrained joy.

But the most surprising joy came my first morning back home. After having been exactly halfway around the world with my internal circadian time-clock operating twelve hours off home time, I awoke at my usual United States time. And, instead of the dreaded jet lag of disorientation and befuddlement, I was lying wide awake in bed praising God. Then joy just flooded the whole room and enwrapped me in itself like the down comforter under which I was snuggling in the Minnesota chill. Joy instead of horrible jet lag!

However, God did not give me that joy by letting me stay home, by not facing me with hard things. He gave it in my obedience. It was the same joy that Jesus surprisingly had in the face of impending death when He said, "These things have I spoken unto you that My joy might remain in you, and that your joy might be full" (John 15:11, NASB).

Jesus left His divine joy with His followers on earth when He went back to heaven. Are you settling for only a quickly evaporating mist or an occasional light shower of joy which barely dampens the surface of a soul parched with anxiety, fear, and apprehension? Or is the fountain of Jesus' effusive joy welling up within you, unrestrained and overflowing? It comes from obedience.

Jesus paid a tremendous price for His obedience to the Father. When agonizing in the Garden of Gethsemane, He *could* have prayed "alternate plan B" instead of submitting to the will of the Father that He go to the cross. He *could* have said, "Father, do You remember that committee meeting You, the Holy Spirit, and I had before the foundation of the world? Do You remember our 'alternate plan B'? It didn't have a cross in it, Father. Why don't we use that plan?" Jesus *could* have said, "Oh, just until we get to Easter morning, Father. I'd be glad to pick up this plan then." As we so frequently do, Jesus *could* have prayed "alternate plan B."

But He did not. He chose to be obedient and bear all the world's sin in His sinless body. "Although He was a Son, He learned obedience from the things which He suffered; and having been made perfect, He became to all those who obey Him the source of eternal salvation" (Heb. 5:8,9, NASB).

Something I have learned to expect is that God frequently uses me to answer the prayer that I have prayed. He expects my obedience in doing and saying those things which, at least partially, will bring about that for which I've prayed.

Peter tells us in 1 Peter 1:14–15, *"As obedient children,* do not be conformed to the former lusts which were yours in your ignorance, but like the Holy One who called you, be holy yourselves also in *all* your behavior" (NASB). And in the forgiving formula of 2 Corinthians 2, Paul says he expects forgiving, comforting, and confirming love to be extended to the one who has grieved them (and us), so that he might put them to the test—"whether you are obedient in *all* things" (v. 9, NASB). The price? Obedience in all things.

Rewards

God's requirements for obedience may be extremely high, but the quality of the reward usually equates with the price of the obedience.

Although God expects a lot, He also has fabulous rewards ready to give to those who obey Him. Jesus told us what many of them are, "Truly I say to you, there is no one who has left house or wife or brothers or parents or children, for the sake of the kingdom of God, who shall not receive many times as much at this time, and in the age to come, eternal life" (Luke 18:29–30, NASB). Yes, rewards on earth today and eternity in heaven. But only for those who obey: "Not everyone who says to Me 'Lord, Lord' will enter the kingdom of heaven; but he who *does the will of My Father* who is in heaven" (Matt. 7:21, NASB).

Jesus also said He, the actual Son of God, would abide in those who keep His commandments (1 John 3:24); and God promised to give the third member of the Trinity, the Holy Spirit, to those who obey Him (Acts 5:32).

Could there be a greater reward than to be regarded by Jesus as His friend? Well, He said, "You are My friends *if* you do what I command you" (John 15:14, NASB). It also is a little shocking to think of what the opposite is—not being Jesus' friend if we don't obey Him!

Then the complete, indescribable circle of the obedient life is summed up by Jesus in John 14:21, "He who has My commandments and keeps them, he it is who loves Me; and he who loves Me shall be loved by My Father, and I will love him, and will disclose Myself to him" (NASB). Rewards!

As I kissed the warm forehead of my sleeping grandbaby recently to say good-bye before leaving for Australia and Guam, I said to her daddy, "The price gets higher every time." True. But so does the reward!

Responses

It is awesome to realize that at the end of our lives we will be the sum total of our responses to God's answers to our prayers, for God has chosen to be limited in His next action by our response to His previous answer.

The final outcome of our lives is decided by a life-long series of responses to God's answers to our prayers. The way we respond to God and then He, in turn, to us actually determines the direction our lives will take.

It would be wonderful if each response to God affected only our lives at that point and no more. But not so. One response triggers the domino principle that affects all the rest of life. A major wrong response slips or hurtles us into the path of lost opportunities and missed spiritual growth, limiting God from taking us down the path He intended and planned for us before the foundation of the world.

As I grow older, it is interesting to look back on what seemed to be my correct responses and wonder "what if" I had not followed God's leading in that initial word from Him. What if I had not obeyed His initial call of "behold, I set before you an open door" (Rev. 3:8), when I sought His face about the original prayer experiment that produced my prayer ministry? What path would I have taken? How far astray might I have gone before He would have given me another chance to respond correctly?

We really do determine our own spiritual growth rate, usefulness in God's program for the world, and new opportunities by the way we respond to Him. At any point, we can hinder or completely stop His divine plan for our lives by our rebellious or inadequate response to His answer. Only in eternity will we get a glimpse of "what might have been" had our responses not thwarted God's plans for us.

But with each step of obedience to God's answer to our prayers, He holds us gently yet firmly in that perfect path He has for us—walking hand in hand with Him. Obedience!

Closing Prayer

Dear Father, I know the plans You have for me are best. Forgive me for all the times I have stubbornly gone my own way. Teach

*me to listen to Your answers to my prayers, and then to obey
exactly what You have told me to do—or not to do. Thank You,
Father, for all the wonderful rewards You have ready for me when
I do obey You.*

In Jesus' name, **Amen.**

12

WHEN GOD ANSWERS . . .

Have a Thankful Heart

What happens when God answers? The ultimate, final response on our part should be to thank Him. No matter how God has answered our prayer, the one thing He expects from us is thankfulness.

People tend to insert their thanksgiving at different places in the prayer process. Some never bother to thank God no matter how great and wonderful the answers He sends. Most people, but not all, are thankful when God answers the way they requested and has given them what they wanted. Then, some Christians have matured enough spiritually to thank Him in spite of how He has answered, trusting His divine wisdom.

But the Bible has an even greater requirement as to where the thanksgiving belongs in the whole prayer process. Philippians 4:6, surprisingly, reads, "Be anxious for nothing, but in everything by prayer and supplication *with thanksgiving* let your *requests* be made unto God" (NASB, emphasis mine).

It is rare indeed to find those who actually put their thanksgiving right in with the request. Few are able to be thankful *while* they are asking, because they are concentrating on the

way they want God to answer. And the deeper the personal
need or hurt, the more difficult it becomes to be thankful
while begging God to intervene. Our minds usually are totally
consumed by the problem, not with thanksgiving, during our
wrestling and striving in prayer. It takes deep maturity indeed
to be able to thank God *before* He answers, to be able to
include the thanks *with* the request!

Attitude of Gratitude

Thanksgiving is a lifestyle. Long before He answers, God
requires an *attitude* of thanksgiving. "Devote yourselves to
prayer, keeping alert in it with *an attitude of* thanksgiving"
(Col. 4:2, NASB).

Our ultimate goal is to be engulfed by, saturated with, and
completely controlled by an attitude of gratitude. Not some
emotional high, or an escape from reality, but the actual living
in a state of thankfulness—before, during, and after we receive
answers to our prayers.

Paul explains in 1 Thessalonians 5:18 that this is not an
option, but it is God's will for us, "In everything give thanks;
for this is God's will for you in Christ Jesus" (NASB). While
we are *in* every situation and while we are praying about
it, we are to be thankful. Thanks should not have to be legis-
lated through God's Word, but it should be the spontaneous
response of our whole being toward Him.

I shivered in my hotel room in Australia one winter Sunday
evening. Chills from a flulike sore throat, plus sitting all that
day in buildings with so much less heat than I was used to
in America, left me miserable. Alone in that room, I kept
getting sicker and sicker. I took a bite of an apple, but my
throat hurt too much to swallow it. And I was scheduled to
speak all day, starting early the next morning!

Knowing that no doctor could cure me fast enough for the
next day's seminar, I just knelt down by my bed to pray.
But I didn't panic, I didn't ask God to get a replacement speaker
ready, I didn't even ask to be healed. No, rather I just stayed
there, kneeling in prayer with my whole being wrapped in
His presence—with feelings of thanks spontaneously flowing
to God for the privilege of once again being absolutely dependent upon Him.

I wasn't asking for or expecting what resulted from that prayer, but, rising from my knees, I was surprised to find my throat completely healed. Filled with an attitude of gratitude!

Our attitude while we are making the request greatly influences the way we handle God's answers to our prayer. When the thanksgiving is there at the time of asking, it completely changes how we respond to God's answer, whatever it may be. Our attitude toward God's answer will be largely dependent upon our attitude toward Him during our request.

I was due to leave Dulles Airport in Washington, D.C., at 5:30, Friday evening, November 2, 1984, on Continental flight #383. But it didn't leave. All the radar had gone out in our whole nation's capital, and nothing was leaving that jammed airport the Friday night before election day until they let our planes limp out, one by one, on the dark runways, hours late. But God had an incredible "just trust Me" lesson waiting.

Since this was the last connection that could get me to San Jose, California, in time for the next morning's seminar, and since I had only a half-hour layover in Denver to catch my plane for San Jose, I called to alert the seminar committee. Then I called my prayer chain at home. But the chances of getting to San Jose looked bleak, in fact, humanly impossible.

As my plane droned on in the night, I scribbled on the back of my flight schedule: "As we approached Denver, the announcement came. 'For those of you who are late for connections, there will be one of our people to assist you as you deplane. Just tell him your destination, and he will tell you your plane's gate number—or—if it's gone!' "

I settled back in my seat, almost snuggling down with a smile inside me. Most of my flight had been spent in prayer—not begging God to make my connection, but praying for tomorrow's seminar, His will in my life, my desire to be His handmaiden, to do only what He wanted me to do.

So it was just continuing our conversation when I prayed, "Oh, God, what an incredible feeling! The *privilege* of once again being totally dependent on You. The privilege of once again completely trusting You."

I continued writing on the back of my flight schedule in the darkened plane as the hours dragged on: "There is no anxiety, no worrying, no what if's. Just the overwhelming security and peace—knowing that God is in absolute control."

Then I was once again quoting to Him, but mostly for me, "Be anxious for nothing, but in everything by prayer and supplication with thanksgiving let your requests be made known to God" (Phil. 4:6, NASB). *"The thankfulness just rolled,"* I wrote.

Even when "their man" sent me to the wrong gate, which was in the opposite direction of mine, the assurance in my heart was still there. Completely out of breath, I dashed back— only to see the door of my plane, which miraculously had waited, being closed, then being opened again. And, as I darted in, to hear the call, "That's the last one!"

I shot a quick glance at my heavenly Father, grinned, and breathed a prayer, "Thanks, Father, I knew You would!"

"Through Him then let us *continually* offer up a sacrifice of praise to God, that is, the fruit of lips that give thanks to His name" (Heb. 13:15, NASB).

Why does God expect us to live continuously with an attitude of thanksgiving? Because He knows how it will be of benefit to us. There is a surprising fringe benefit from a lifestyle of thankfulness. A medical doctor in Michigan said with great wisdom that the best way to handle stress is with an "attitude of gratitude." An Old Testament proverb agrees: "A joyful heart is good medicine" (Prov. 17:22, NASB). Why? Because there evidently are chemicals released in our bodies from such an attitude. The single best way to remove stress from life, the doctor had wisely concluded, is an *attitude of gratitude*.

In Advance

When we leave a lovely dinner party or a special vacation time with a friend, we often say, "Thanks *for* everything." Also, after God has sent us successes and victories, we tend to say the same to Him. And this is good and scriptural, for Ephesians 5:20 does tell us to be thankful *for* all things. But the real test of our relationship with God is being able to say sincerely, "Thank You," *before* He gives us anything. To be able to say, "Thanks for everything," by our whole lifestyle of gratitude and by our prayer requests including "thanks in advance."

How is this possible? It is through a *relationship with the Father.* Frequently, our thanksgiving *for* God's answer comes from circumstances that have been changed by God or when He has removed the trial, illness, or heartache in answer to our praying; but thankfulness during the request requires a relationship of unequivocal trust in God that what He will answer will be right and best.

It almost seemed as though God was putting me to the test recently one morning before dawn. Our daughter Nancy was more than two weeks overdue, and her doctor had decided to start the procedure to bring the baby on that day.

I had watched Nancy getting larger and larger as her unborn baby became less and less active—exactly as it had been with my two handicapped babies; and, just two weeks before, we had watched our Jan dangerously lose half her blood giving birth to her Crista. The apprehension and anxiety were growing in me. I remembered Nancy's Cindy with the cord wrapped three times around her neck at birth, and the possibility of what might go wrong with this birth loomed menacingly.

"Lord," I cried, "how can I thank You in advance with all these concerns in my heart?" I knew the scriptural teachings well, yet applying them at a time like this was not easy. But then God so clearly brought Philippians 4:6 into my mind, and I lay in the predawn blackness reciting over and over, "Be anxious for nothing, but in everything by prayer . . . *with thanksgiving* let your requests be made known to God" (Phil. 4:6, NASB, emphasis mine).

Suddenly, unsolicited, the thanksgiving welled up within me and permeated my entire being and, it seemed, the whole bedroom. My furrowed forehead automatically gave way to the smile that came. My eyes were moist with tears—of thanksgiving!

What had happened? Somehow, my focus changed direction—from possible earthly, human problems—to God. The thanks to Him just flowed. Who He is! He never makes a mistake. It is He who will take that child from the womb! And Kathleen Mae finally arrived—healthy and beautiful.

Who God Is

Last week God showed me a secret of being able to thank Him right at the time of my requests. I had just asked Him to help me praise and thank Him more, and I was reading through the Psalms for specific wordings of praise and thanks-giving, when He stopped me on 7:17, "I will give thanks to the Lord according to *His* righteousness" (NASB, emphasis mine).

According to. There it is again, that little prepositional phrase. I am to thank God, not according to my righteousness, nor my pastor's, nor my parents', but according to *His* righteousness.

But what is God's righteousness? It is the quality of actually *being* right and just, and then of being this way in His treatment of His creatures. Thus, I can know unequivocally that what God answers is right and just, and I can trust His answers unquestioningly. Then I can thank Him while I ask, not according to what I want or what I desire, but according to who He is—righteous—in His dealings with me.

Also, God's righteousness is without prejudice or partiality. Other people's responses to my requests are influenced by their attitudes toward me. But not God's. He answers my prayers without any unfair prejudice against me or harmful indulgence toward me. So I can be secure in His answers.

God's righteousness is His holiness as it affects us—His transitive holiness. Since His holiness is the chief subject of rejoicing and adoration in heaven, when I give thanks unto the Lord according to His righteousness, I actually am joining the attitude and activities of those in heaven—rejoicing and adoring Him.

Frequently, prisoners who accept Christ while incarcerated tell me that they have prayed, "Oh, God, get me out of this hell-hole." Then they expected God to answer their prayer with a miraculous pardon, change in a parole law, or some other divine intervention. Now, God has done this occasionally, but usually He has answered no to that prayer. Then their response to His no has been, "If that's the kind of God I'm serving now, I don't want anything to do with Him any more. He let me down." However, I'm surprised how frequently inmates, who have recently become Christians, share with me that they already have grasped who God is, that He knows what He is doing, and it is for their ultimate good—and that they can trust Him completely. Then their response to God's no answer to that prayer has been, "Thanks, God, for leaving me here. You have a purpose. What is it?"

There is a difference in thanking God for what He does

and who He is. It is easy and almost natural to thank Him when He answers our prayers with something obviously good or what we wanted. But it is not as easy to thank Him for being what He is—right and just—before He answers.

Faith in Who God Is

Thanking God in advance takes not only knowing who He is but an unshakable faith in the God to whom we are praying. Only when this adequate view of God has been arrived at *before* making the request can this attitude of thanksgiving be there *during* the request.

Actually, we have been practicing this principle in our prayer seminars for years. After teaching the participants who God really is (He never makes a mistake and does all things for our good), I ask them to pray aloud in small groups, giving God the most important thing in the whole world to them right then. The next prayer is thanking Him—in advance— before they have any idea what He might decide to do with what they just gave Him. This thanksgiving prayer is only possible because they have firmly grasped who God really is.

In my seminars, I always pray what I expect the audience to pray. Last March, I had just asked the audience to give that most important material or human possession, relation- ship, or circumstance to God when I knew I had to pray a very difficult prayer. We were expecting our second set of grandbabies in five months, and I knew I had to give God the thing I wanted more than anything in the world right then—two healthy, normal babies!

I struggled, momentarily remembering the heartache of my own two spina bifida babies. But this was erased from my mind almost immediately as a spirit of thankfulness welled up within me. Thankfulness for all the wonderful lessons and gains God had given me through those two babies. And, with unequivocal assurance in my heart that God is right and just, I gave these precious, unborn wee ones to God—for anything He knew to be best—according to His righteousness.

It was the following July when God assured my heart with Psalm 100:3, "It is He who has made us, and not we ourselves." And I marked it in my Bible with a huge asterisk in the margin.

Then His next words to me were from the fifth verse, "For the Lord is good; His lovingkindness is everlasting" (NASB). Tears burst into my eyes as I cried, "Babies. I *can* trust His lovingkindness." Who God is!

Our Jan phoned one day announcing, "Mother, I was talking to my friend Diane last night and I have something for your new book. They want another baby so badly, but she just had her second miscarriage. But she told me she is actually thanking God for this miscarriage, because He knows exactly which egg He wants fertilized to produce their next baby. It is a deep-down attitude of thankfulness she has, not just words." I listened in awe.

"Mother," Jan continued, "it isn't when people say, 'I will be thankful because the Bible says I must be.' But real thankfulness depends on who is in control of your life. Who is in the driver's seat of your life. Who is sovereign. This is what produces joy in all circumstances, Mother. When you see God as sovereign and never making a mistake, you can thank Him for whatever happens—even a second miscarriage when you desperately want a baby."

David had an incredibly accurate view of who God is. And it produced his beautiful prayer of thanksgiving:

> So David blessed the Lord in the sight of all the assembly; and David said, "Blessed are Thou, O Lord God of Israel our Father, forever and ever. Thine, O Lord, is the greatness and the power and the glory and the victory and the majesty, indeed everything that is in the heavens and the earth; Thine is the dominion, O Lord, and Thou dost exalt Thyself as head over all. Both riches and honor come from Thee, and Thou dost rule over all, and in Thy hand is power and might; and it lies in Thy hand to make great, and to strengthen everyone. Now *therefore,* our God, *we thank Thee,* and praise Thy glorious name" (1 Chron. 29:10–13, NASB, emphasis mine).

David's word *therefore* explains his whole prayer. "Therefore"—because of who You, God, really are—we thank Thee.

Who God is. With no environment and no heredity, God alone chose who He would be. He alone decided what He would dedicate and consecrate Himself to be. Then He revealed it to us through His Word and His involvement in our lives so that we, with David, also could explode with our prayers of thanksgiving.

Keep Alert

But occasionally, I have trouble and slip from thankfulness into grumbling. It was at one of those times in August of 1984, while on vacation, that I recognized this attitude in me while reading Colossians 4:2, "Devote yourselves to prayer, keeping alert in it with an *attitude of thanksgiving"* (NASB). Deeply rebuked, I cried out, "Oh, God, forgive me. Bring me back to a right relationship with You. Make my testimony positive before others. I have taken my eyes off You. Replace my uptightness with your peace and joy—and thankfulness!" And it worked—as it always does!

Why do we have to keep alert in prayer? Because the Bible clearly tells us that Christians are in a spiritual battle and that we have an enemy, Satan.

In Ephesians 6, God describes the armor that will enable us to stand firm against the devil. But most of the time, we stop short of God's warning at the close, to be on the alert— *in prayer.* Verse 18 cautions: "With all prayer and petition pray at all times in the Spirit, and with this in view, be on the alert with all perseverance and petition for all the saints."

Obviously, Satan wants us to grumble, to be negative and powerless, thus destroying our own well-being and witness. However, being alert isn't one of the things we usually associate with prayer. But God does. He expects us to be fighting the only battle known where the soldiers go forth on their knees.

In, With, For

Thanking God *in* everything (1 Thess. 5:18) and *with* our requests (Phil. 4:6) does not cancel out His command to thank Him *for* everything. All three of these prepositions describe a relationship of the pray-er to God, which are commanded in the Bible.

God must be horrified at how ungrateful His children can be for His answers. A woman who had been in a wheelchair for years walked spryly up to me at a large denomination's weekend retreat last month. She complained bitterly to me that she could not get any faith in God—even after He had miraculously healed her in answer to prayer, and she had not had to use her wheelchair since. I cringed at her inability to thank God *for* something as spectacular as that.

We are shocked at the nine out of ten lepers Jesus healed who did not bother to come back to thank Him, but I wonder what our ratio is today—even when He answers with exactly what we requested. Is it more than one out of ten?

Ephesians 5:20 says that God expects us to be thankful *for* His answer, no matter how He answers our prayer—even when it is not what we wanted. "Always giving thanks *for* all things in the name of our Lord Jesus Christ to God, even the Father" (NASB). Then *always* giving thanks every time—even when we had asked for something different. His answers are the source of our praise and thanks, no matter how our opinions differ from God's.

A friend, Ruth Johnson Jay, wrote me a note several years ago in which she expressed her thanks to the Lord for a pair of crutches! She had just completed thirty years with the Back to the Bible broadcasts when she wrote, "I fell, broke my ankle in three places and dislocated the bone. Surgery was necessary . . . but I even find myself thanking the Lord for crutches. I cannot put any weight on the cast for four to six weeks, and none (on the foot) after that for another four weeks. So you can see why I am thanking the Lord for crutches!"

I'm sure that another reason why we don't thank God *for* His answer is that frequently we don't recognize events and gifts *as* answers to our prayers. We just take His bountiful supply or dramatic action for granted when it comes. This is one reason I teach my prayer seminar participants to write down their prayer request and then what happened so they can put the two together. How often I hear their surprised, "Oh, that *was* His answer!"

Even worse, of course, is when God answers and we have forgotten that we even prayed. Keeping a list of our requests helps tremendously here, also. Then a periodic reading through the list of requests can be quite revealing: "Oh, yes, that provision, healing, or circumstance really *was* an answer to one of my prayers!" Then the thankfulness for it comes.

There also are those times when I believe God deliberately waits long enough to answer so that there will be no doubt who gets the credit for what happens. It is only when I have exhausted all human resources that He finally answers—so that I will recognize the answer as coming from Him. And thank Him for it. And give Him all the glory!

Thanks For

The list of things *for* which I thank God in my prayers would fill many books, but here are just a few:

For redemption. Thanking God for transferring me out of the state of sin into which I was born into His glorious kingdom—forgiven and bound for eternity with my beloved Savior. "Joyously giving thanks to the Father, who has qualified us to share in the inheritance of the saints in light. For He delivered us from the domain of darkness, and transferred us to the kingdom of His beloved Son, in whom we have redemption, the forgiveness of sins" (Col. 1:11–14, NASB).

For peace. Thanking God for the formula which has produced peace in my life. Here it is: "Be anxious for nothing, but in everything by prayer and supplication with thanksgiving let your requests be made known to God. And [then] the peace of God, which surpasses all comprehension shall guard your hearts and your minds in Christ Jesus" (Phil. 4:6, NASB). The prerequisite, usually omitted as we try to claim this promised peace, is a lifestyle of an attitude of gratitude—before, during, and after the prayer requests. But the whole formula really works.

For His omniscience. Although there are more than four billion people on planet earth, God the Father can give His undivided attention to each one of them all the time. So, although I'm just 1/4,000,000,000 of the world's population, God watches over me, sorts through the intents of my heart, listens and cares when I cry for help, never makes a mistake in His moment-by-moment guiding of my life, and will judge me according to His righteousness.

For Jesus' blood. Almost daily, I thank God that the blood of Jesus is the only positively irresistible force against evil. For many years, He has proved in my life that there is no immovable object from Satan that the irresistible force of His precious blood—once and for all victorious on the cross—cannot and will not dislodge and wash away. "Now the salvation, and the power, and the kingdom of our God and the authority of His Christ have come, for the accuser of our brethren has been thrown down, who accuses them before our God day and night. And they overcame him because of the blood of the Lamb" (Rev. 12:10, 11, NASB).

For setting me free. "If therefore the Son shall make you free, you shall be free indeed" (John 8:36, NASB). How grateful

I am for Jesus' promise that I could be free *in* all circumstances—not *from* them. No intellectual bondage, no spiritual enslavement because of sin, no confinement of my spirit because of a wheelchair or a hospital bed, no restriction of my vision in a nursing home room, no mental imprisonment to others' ideologies, no emotional enslavement to those who would demand my will, no restraint of spiritual insight and hope because of a weakened body. No imprisonment of the real me—because Jesus has set me free.

For God using my body. For the progressively growing thankfulness of having given God my body in 1965, in that once-for-all action of Romans 12:1. For frequently being healed but, much more important, for the privilege of having God always take all the anxiety out of bodily infirmities. Thanks for His replacement of that anxiety with absolute trust in Him as the One who owns, is in charge of, and is responsible for my body.

But even more, I am thankful for the privilege of God using my still-living sacrifice in any way He chooses—to teach others the power of their prayers for me, that the works of God might be displayed in me (as in the man born blind whom Jesus healed), or to lead someone to Jesus in a redemptive way because of watching His power to transcend and use me through, and in spite of, physical weaknesses.

For you, dear prayer partners. I "do not cease giving thanks for you, while making mention of you in my prayers" (Eph. 1:16, NASB). You who have prayed diligently, faithfully, and sacrificially for me year after year, and seeing God answering with wisdom, courage, and sometimes supernatural strength—I bow in humble thanksgiving and gratitude to God for you.

"And He will yet deliver us, you also joining in helping us through your prayers, that thanks may be given by many persons on our behalf for the favor bestowed upon us through the prayers of many" (2 Cor. 1:10, 11, NASB). Your prayers!

Preserved and Enhanced

What happens when God answers? After all God does with and through His answers to prayer, He still has a final step. He does not discard them after answering, but preserves and enhances them in heaven: "And when He [the Lamb] had taken the book, the four living creatures and the twenty-four elders fell down before the Lamb, having each one a harp, and golden bowls full of incense, which are the prayers of the saints" (Rev. 5:8, NASB).

"MY PRAYERS!!!" I wrote in the margin by that Bible verse. "I am one of God's saints—true believers in Jesus Christ. My prayers didn't disappear when God answered them! No, they are preserved in heaven!"

"And this is the song they sang before Jesus the Lamb," I continued to write, "holding *my* prayers": "Worthy are Thou to take the book, and to break its seals; for Thou wast slain, and didst purchase for God with Thy blood men from every tribe and tongue and people and nation. And Thou hast made them to be a kingdom and priests to our God; and they will reign upon the earth" (Rev. 5:9, 10, NASB).

Then, joined by millions of angels, they said with a loud voice: "Worthy is the Lamb that was slain to receive power and riches and wisdom and might and honor and glory and blessing" (Rev. 5:12, NASB).

Still holding my prayers and yours, they were joined by every created thing which is in heaven and on the earth and under the earth and on the sea, all saying: "To Him who sits on the throne, and to the Lamb, be blessing and honor and glory and dominion forever and ever" (Rev. 5:13, NASB).

I wept as I realized all the agonizing, wrestling, and tears; all the praise, worship, submission, and intercessory prayers from my whole life are there. Not lost, or cast aside once they are answered—but preserved for eternity.

Yes, the final reason for our thanksgiving in the prayer process is that God has chosen only special words of ours— our prayers—to keep forever.

But even more astounding, they not only will be preserved— but enhanced! Enhanced by the grace and cost of the vessels that hold them. The apostle John on the Isle of Patmos, as he was penning these things to come, saw our preserved prayers in precious, valuable golden bowls. Broad, shallow, saucer-like bowls, made of the most precious commodity known on earth in that day—costly gold.

Then the final scene in the long journey of our prayers' life is recorded in Revelation 8:3-4. When all the seals are broken on that book in the Lamb's hands, this climactic celestial scene will unfold:

And another angel came and stood at the altar, holding a golden censer; and much incense was given to him, that he might add it to the prayers of all the saints upon the golden altar which was before the throne. And the smoke of the incense, *with the prayers of the saints, went up before God* out of the angel's hand (NASB, emphasis mine).

"Oh, God, I am not worthy!" my heart cried. "Thank You, Lord!"

How wonderful to know that—after all the other things that have happened to us and to those for whom we pray, through God's answers to prayers—there is one more thing. God feels every one of them is important enough to preserve— and precious enough to enhance—in golden bowls before His throne.

When we get to heaven, will we be embarrassed at how few prayers of ours God received to put in golden bowls? And of those He did get, will their content bring a blush to our cheeks? Selfish prayers—to glorify ourselves, to be consumed on our lusts? "Grocery lists" of our endless wants?

Or will we be overwhelmed at the sight of them all—preserved because of their permanent significance in God's sight? And we will suddenly realize that prayer has been one of God's chief means of accomplishing His will on earth—our prayers!

What happens when God answers prayer? He pulls back the curtain to the next act of our lives. And, through His answer, lets us step into that next room of our lives—open doors, spiritual maturity, accomplishing His will on planet earth. One step nearer to the Christlikeness He had planned for us before the foundation of the world.

And when we finally take that last step into God's throne room, our prayers will be there—waiting for us—with our Lord Himself.